MW00463509

"You have worked hard for many years to build your business, it's successful but it's just not fun anymore. How do you stop doing the things you don't enjoy, focus on the things you love, and reduce the amount of time you spend on your business without sacrificing your income and all the value that you have created? The answer is: read this book. Jim's six-step system outlines exactly what you need to do to get your life back and keep your business."

— John Spence, one of the top business and leadership experts in the world

HALF-RETIRE

Keep Your Business,
Ditch the Stress

JIM MUEHLHAUSEN, JD

A SAVIO REPUBLIC BOOK
An Imprint of Post Hill Press
ISBN: 978-1-64293-565-3
ISBN (eBook): 978-1-64293-566-0

Half-Retire:
Keep Your Business, Ditch the Stress
© 2020 by Jim Muehlhausen, JD

Cover Design by David Ter-Avanesyan
Interior images provided by Jim Muehlhausen, JD

posthillpress.com
New York · Nashville
Published in the United States of America

In my previous books, I used this icon to denote a "Mulekick." As you might imagine, with a last name like Muehlhausen, your nickname in high school is "mule." When you gently or not-so-gently prod people for a living, you can call them shoves or kicks. Combine them, and you have a Mulekick. I will use this icon to denote counterintuitive thinking, key points, or the not-so-gentle shove you may need.

Throughout this book you will see the terms Half-Retire®, Half-Retired™, Half-Retirement™, Half-Retiree™, and Half-Retiring™. All of these terms are used with our trademark, reserved, whether denoted or not, and refer to the person or process of Half-Retiring.

Other trademarked terms in the book may not include the ™ notation for better readability, but all rights are reserved regardless of denotation or lack thereof.

TABLE OF CONTENTS

INTRODUCTION

"RETIREMENT? YEAH, THAT would be great, but I can't see it happening any time soon."

During the thousands of one-on-one meetings that I've had with small and medium-sized business owners over the years, I've encountered this situation more times than I can count. They're getting up in age, and they're tired of the daily grind, but they have a massive pit in their stomach when they think about retirement. Many are worried they will be bored if they retire. Even more know that they can't sell their business for enough to maintain their lifestyle—so they just keep on working and ignore that pit.

At some point, we all need a "Graceful Exit" from our business. I define a Graceful Exit as one where the stress of business ownership is removed: You get to spend your time however you want and you have enough money to do it. Selling your business for a big pile of money can be a Graceful Exit. Passing the business to your kids can be a Graceful Exit. Shutting the doors and walking away can be a Graceful Exit if you have enough money to live your life already. As long as you can do what you want to, how you want to, and have no financial stress after your exit, it is graceful.

The reason many business owners are feeling that pit in their stomach is that they know, deep down, that they don't have the ability to Gracefully Exit the business.

The good news is that there's a new way to Gracefully Exit your business. It's called Half-Retire. When you Half-Retire, you keep your current business income but shift from hard-earned income to equity income. You can ditch the stress and work as much or as little as you'd like doing only the work you enjoy.

Sound too good to be true?

I've seen many business owners create better family relationships, live an enviable lifestyle, and have plenty of income by not selling their business and Half-Retiring instead. This book will show you the process you can follow to do the same.

The Half-Retire system enables you to move your business from the daily grind to harvesting all the rewards of your years of hard work. After all the hard work you have put in, you deserve to fully reap the rewards your business can provide. Half-Retirement will help you extract all the value from that hard work. Half-Retire hyper-leverages your key talents, refocuses your team, and ensures that every component of your business is scalable and reproducible. Ultimately, it enables you to cut down on your stress, reduce the number of hours you work, increase the price buyers are willing to pay for your business in the near future, and retire completely when you are ready.

CHAPTER 1

IF I DIDN'T OWN THIS PLACE, I'D QUIT

A CLIENT BLURTED this out inadvertently during a meeting and it really stuck with me. Every business owner in the world, including myself, has felt this way. As we head into our Enjoyment Years, our tolerance for B.S. goes down, and we find ourselves daydreaming about the magic button that makes the headaches of business owner- ship go away. Of course, there is no magic button, but I hope to show you the closest thing to it. Half-Retirement.

I don't like the term Golden Years, because it makes me feel 107 years old. I will use the term Enjoyment Years to describe the well-deserved time you should be taking to do activities outside work that bring you happiness.

For many of us, owning and running our own business is a big part of the American Dream. According to a survey from *Entrepreneur*, the majority of Americans would like to be their own bosses, if they aren't already.[1] Why do so many people prefer the stress and responsibility of entrepreneurship over earning a reliable paycheck every two weeks?

If you're like me, working nine to five every single day just doesn't appeal to you. You like being able to set your own schedule without getting stuck doing the same thing all day, every day. You don't mind taking some risks and having life be a little unpredictable. In fact—some days anyway—you actually find it exhilarating.

Plus, once a business is off the ground, there are countless benefits to being the owner. You have a steady income stream, and you get to hire and work with people you like in an industry you care about. And you rarely, if ever, suffer from being bored!

Yet no matter what anyone says, there are also drawbacks. More often than not, the success of the company—and all its employees—rides on your decisions, your performance, and your judgment. You carry all that on your shoulders, even when you try to get away.

In the course of over ten thousand one-on-one coaching sessions with business owners, I saw a recurring problem with no real solution. Many were ready to retire or at least cut back, but when they decided to sell, the fair market value of their company was not enough to replace their income. I saw them either settle for pennies on the dollar in a sale, or keep working and miss out on the life they really wanted.

It Doesn't Seem Fair

It doesn't seem fair that business owners' years of hard work are not better rewarded. I studied business owners struggling to gracefully exit their business and found a group of them who had found a way to "cash out" of their business without selling it. They kept

---

1   "Expectations vs. Reality" (January 15, 2018). Retrieved from: http://news. vistaprint.com/expectations-vs-reality.

their business income but removed themselves from the daily grind. I began studying these owners and painstakingly analyzed what they did and how they did it. By distilling hundreds of best practices, combining their formulas for success, and augmenting them with my experience, I created the Half-Retire System.

> **Half-Retirement transforms your business from a source of working income to a source of income earned from your equity in the business. It creates a new and unique Exit Strategy, and it enables you to enjoy all the benefits of business ownership without the burdens, by letting you keep the income stream and leadership role, while losing the stress.**

Thousands of Half-Retirees around the country are already benefitting from working fewer hours and doing more of what they love to do. They've figured out how to keep their income, company car, entertainment budget, social connections, and CEO status, too. But before we get into the nuts and bolts of how this can work for you, let's take a closer look at the challenges most business owners face on a day-to-day basis.

The Myth of Flexibility

One of the most appealing parts of being your own boss is maintaining a flexible schedule, but the ugly truth is that just because you're not working nine to five doesn't mean you're not working seven to eleven. In fact, most business owners and entrepreneurs work far *more* than forty hours a week, not less. Accurate numbers are incredibly hard to come by, but several studies indicate that well over half the CEOs of small and medium-sized businesses put in more than full-time hours, and less than 5 percent work that coveted thirty hours a week or less.[2] Perhaps most importantly, **80 percent of business owners report feeling like they work too much.** That might be okay when you're twenty-five, but not so great thirty years later.

If many business owners choose their path because they value flexibility, why do so many get stuck working around the clock? I'm guessing you already know the answer. It takes an incredible amount of time and effort to run a successful business, especially at first. In fact, in the early years of a new venture, a willingness to put in the long days may be what makes the difference between staying afloat or closing your doors.

Some of the most successful entrepreneurs agree. Author and entrepreneur Grant Cardone reports regularly working ninety-five hours a week,[3] and Gary Vaynerchuk says you should be ready to work eighteen hours a day at least for your business's first year.[4] The business owners who make it far enough to even think about retiring are often the ones who have been willing to pay their dues with years of late nights and skipped vacations.

But it doesn't always end when your company is off the ground. In some ways, the more successful a business becomes, the more attention it demands. Robust sales growth is awesome, but it brings its own set of challenges. At the very least, you have to hire and deal with the associated human resources issues. You might also have

---

2   "Survey Shows Work-Life Balance is Possible, Not Likely for Entrepreneurs," *The Alternative Board* (November 8, 2013). Retrieved from: https://www. thealternativeboard.com/new-survey-shows-work-life-balance-is-possible-but-not-likely-for-entrepreneurs/.

3   Kathleen Elkins, "Self-made millionaire: If you want to get rich, start working 95 hours a week," CNBC (December 5, 2016). Retrieved from: https:// www.cnbc.com/2016/12/05/self-made-millionaire-if-you-want-to-get-rich-start-working-95-hours-a-week.html.

4   Gary Vaynerchuk, "Why Startup Founders Need to Set Aside 18 Hours a Day for the First Year" (November 25, 2015). Retrieved from: https://www.inc. com/gary-vaynerchuk/askgaryvee-episode-90-18-hours-a-day.html.

to find and build out new office or factory space. Before you know it, decades are passing, your kids are growing up, and you've never quite made it to that flexible schedule you envisioned when you got started.

There's absolutely nothing wrong with making short-term sacrifices—even for years—to achieve long-term goals. The problem is that many business owners find the routine of long hours and endless workweeks almost impossible to escape. Some actually seem to thrive on it. Cardone himself declared, "If you gave me $5 billion, I'd still be grinding tomorrow."[5]

For the rest of us, we are looking for a way to cut back on the most draining demands of our business so we can enjoy the spoils of our many years building the business. At some point, you want the treadmill to slow down a bit, but many find it hard to decrease their speed without falling face first into the treadmill. You realize, if you slow down, something will come apart in the business, and it's just not worth trying. So you keep running full speed and fall asleep watching television every night.

The Dark Side of Entrepreneurship

Can you live a balanced, healthy life if you're working nonstop? Only you can answer that for yourself, but a growing body of research confirms that working long hours for years takes a toll on us mentally, physically, emotionally, and personally. It's not my job to tell you what to do, but I will give you the facts: the overwhelming majority of people cannot work all the time without paying a serious long-term price.

---

5   Kathleen Elkins, "Self-made millionaires agree on how many hours you should be working to succeed," CNBC (June 15, 2017). Retrieved from: https://www.cnbc.com/2017/06/15/self-made-millionaires-agree-on-how-many-hours-you-should-be-working.html.

Mental and Physical Health

Most business owners are stressed out,[6] and for many, this stress adversely affects their quality of life.[7] Why are business owners and entrepreneurs so much more likely than the rest of the population to suffer from adverse psychological conditions? The answer is way too complicated for us to tackle here, so let's just look at one factor: **sleep.** According to multiple studies, sleep deprivation is strongly correlated with poor mental health.[8] And guess what? Business owners and CEOs are notorious for not getting enough sleep![9]

Chronic sleep deprivation also carries the risk of a myriad of physical illnesses, including high blood pressure, heart disease, obesity, and diabetes.[10] Some business owners may move around a factory floor or office space during the day, but others risk settling into a sedentary lifestyle, spending hours at a time in front of their computers. And all of us have probably eaten too much junk food as we struggle to grab meals on the go.

---

6   According to a 2015 study conducted by scholars at UC-Berkeley and UC-San Francisco, 72 percent of entrepreneurs studied had mental health concerns, with half reporting a lifetime mental condition, and a third reporting two lifetime conditions. Michael A. Freeman, Sheri L. Johnson, Paige J. Staudenmaier, and Mackenzie R. Zisser, "Are Entrepreneurs 'Touched with Fire'?" (April 17, 2015). Retrieved from: http://www.michaelafreemanmd.com/Research_files/Are%20Entrepreneurs%20Touched%20with%20Fire%20(pre-pub%20n)%204-17-15.pdf.

7   The conditions reported by entrepreneurs included depression, anxiety, and ADHD. By comparison, just 18.5 percent of the general population in the United States experiences at least one mental health condition in a given year. See: "Any Mental Illness (AMI) Among Adults" (updated February 2019). Retrieved from: http://www.nimh.nih.gov/health/statistics/prevalence/any-mental-illness-ami-among-adults.shtml.

8   "Sleep and mental health: Sleep deprivation can affect your mental health," *Harvard Health Publications* (June 18, 2018). Retrieved from: https://www.health.harvard.edu/newsletter_article/sleep-and-mental-health.

9   Anna Johansson, "Why Aren't Entrepreneurs Getting Enough Sleep?" *Entrepreneur* (June 7, 2017). Retrieved from: https://www.entrepreneur.com/article/295395.

10   "How is the body affected by sleep deprivation?" National Institute of Child Health and Human Development. Retrieved from: https://www.nichd.nih.gov/health/topics/sleep/conditioninfo/inadequate-sleep.

There are plenty of other factors that come with running a business that can wear us down. Successful business owners take risks, assume huge responsibilities, push through endless obstacles, work at a breakneck pace, and are constantly solving complex problems. All this can be pretty tolerable when we're younger, but eventually, the stress catches up with us.

Personal Relationships

Common sense reminds us that working nonstop will take a toll on our personal relationships. While divorce is hardly exclusive to entrepreneurs, the life of a business owner puts unique strains on both marriage and parenting. Healthy family relationships require an investment of time and energy, and too often, business owners are short on both.

In addition to consuming much of business owners' free time, the emotional and financial strains associated with running a business can wear on the important people in their lives as well. Even when they do make time for that quiet dinner at a favorite restaurant, they may talk about work throughout the evening, making spouses or partners feel unimportant or ignored. Any of that sound familiar?

Furthermore, some of the personal qualities that help you start a successful business may make you difficult to deal with as a spouse or parent. You may need drive, decisiveness, and a willingness to take risks to launch your company, but your spouse may need you to be reliable, understanding, and willing to compromise. As one author puts it, "The entrepreneurial spirit has great characteristics for those who want to achieve success in business. However, these same characteristics can be the very downfall of that entrepreneur's marriage [and family]."[11]

---

11   Chirag Kulkarni, "The Toughest Job an Entrepreneur Has Is to Keep Their Marriage Together," *Huffington Post* (September 13, 2017). Retrieved from: https://www.huffingtonpost.com/entry/the-toughest-job-an-entrepreneur-has-is-to-keep-their_us_59b97a37e4b02c642e4a1352.

I have decades-long relationships with many of my clients, so I know their significant others. You would be surprised how many times I have heard a loved one tell me that they resent or hate the business. The most shocking admission was a wife that said she wished the business would burn down. I bring this up to remind you, and myself, that loved ones put up with a lot from business owners like us.

The challenge with running a business and being a parent often boils down to time and attention as well. Unlike many nine-to-five jobs, businesses are unpredictable. But so are children. As one mother put it, "[There's a] constant pull of wanting to spend time with my daughter, attend her school functions, and supervise field trips versus the pull of wanting to run a business that I'm proud of and not let my partners, employees, and clients down."[12]

That Elusive Work-Life Balance

Business owners may genuinely love what they do, but that doesn't mean that running their company should be their only source of meaning and purpose. In fact, many of the world's most innovative business leaders are equally passionate about hobbies that have nothing to do with their industries. From playing chess or musical instruments to athletic and outdoor pursuits, these leaders find a

---

12   Susan Lamotte, "The Unique Challenges of Being a Parent and an Entrepreneur," *Fast Company* (June 15, 2015). Retrieved from: https://www.fastcompany.com/3047191/the-unique-challenges-of-being-a-parent-and-an-entrepreneur.

wide variety of interests to relieve stress, stimulate creativity, and enrich their lives.

But where can we find the time for this kind of recreation? Some entrepreneurs take vacations, but others rarely do, worrying about things falling apart in their absence. Even when they do get away, they often bring the laptop and the cell phone, working in a new location, but not really getting the downtime they need.

What do you like to do when you actually have free time? How often do you get to do it? Don't just give it a cursory thought. Stop for a moment and think. Entrepreneurs are so busy entrepreneuring that they forget how to dream about much outside of business objectives. If the business ran perfectly without any work required from you, what would you do?

If you're happy with the time you are able to devote to your hobbies and outside interests, then maybe you don't need to make any major changes in the way you run your business. But if you wish you had more time to check things off your bucket list, golf, hike, paint, or play in a band, you don't want to wait until you're too old to enjoy it to start.

My Story

Can you imagine starting a business during the Great Depression? That's exactly what my grandfather did. Not only did the company survive conditions that destroyed countless businesses that might have been viable in a more favorable economic climate, but by the time I was born, it was also a multimillion-dollar enterprise.

I grew up watching my father and uncles drive nice cars, live in nice houses, and have flexible schedules, all thanks to that company that Grandpa built. But I wasn't just drawn to the perks. I was a naturally ambitious and energetic kid, and I just couldn't wait to get out there and work in the business myself.

Grandpa's company was the most exciting place in the world to me, and I just knew I would be running the whole thing one day. By thirteen, I had persuaded my father to fudge my age so I could work right out there on the factory floor. I started out on the machines, but by the next summer, I'd been promoted. Soon I was doing grown-up work, like calling around the country to get quotes from suppliers, writing computer programs, and job costing.

I went away to college convinced I'd be ready to take over everything by the time I graduated. Unfortunately, I don't think I made my plans clear enough to my relatives. I came home with my accounting degree and CPA certification—fully prepared to take the reins of the company—only to discover that they had sold it right out from under me! My older relatives all got a nice check, of course, but I was out of a job.

Unsure of what to do next, I went to law school. But after one semester, I still heard the business world calling my name. So, together with a college friend, I bought a car repair franchise. I wasn't a car guy or even mechanically inclined, but it still felt way more natural to me than being a lawyer. Within a few years, we had expanded to three stores and eventually sold them off after I graduated from law school, because I had correctly anticipated a significant deterioration in market conditions.

Then I started a manufacturing company, which I ran for nearly a decade with all the successes and pains common to business owners. When I sold the company, I began creating business owner mastermind groups and advising CEOs around the world, which ultimately gave rise to the Half-Retire system.

Why not Retire Tomorrow?

Despite the harm that working too much can do, many Americans are continuing to work until even later in life. While the average retirement age for women has held steady, for men, it has been rising since the 1980s.[13] Today, many Americans can expect to work full time until age seventy or even beyond.

Of course, there are many understandable reasons to postpone retirement past the traditional age of sixty-five. First of all, Americans are living longer. When Social Security was established in 1935, the average life expectancy was just sixty-one years, so most Americans never even lived long enough to receive their benefits. Today, the average life expectancy is nearly eighty. This is great news, but it means we have to figure out how to pay for those fifteen, twenty, or even thirty years of retirement. This new reality, combined with fewer workers receiving the generous pensions that were once the mainstay of a white-collar job, demands much more careful financial planning than most of our grandparents had to worry about.

Second, most entrepreneurs plan to sell their businesses to fund a large portion of their retirement. But, as we will detail extensively in the pages that follow, far too many cannot currently get the sale price they need in order to retire comfortably. This is a major reason many owners keep working, even if they feel ready to stop or at least slow down.

Third, many business owners take their role as the leader of their team seriously and feel responsible for the employees who have helped them achieve their dreams. They may postpone retirement, even if they can get a good price for their business, because they are concerned that a new owner will either fire their employees or not treat them well. This is certainly an admirable reason to keep going, but since none of us will live forever, it's really just postponing the inevitable.

Fourth, there are some owners who are ready to sell for the right price and feel confident about their employees' fate, but they are simply unable to disentangle themselves from the day-to-day

---

13   Alicia H. Munnell, "Why the Average Retirement Age is Rising," *Market Watch* (October 15, 2017). Retrieved from: https://www.marketwatch.com/story/why-the-average-retirement-age-is-rising-2017-10-09.

workings of the business. Too much of what goes on all day relies on their physical presence, so they don't know how to even begin the transition.

And of course, not everyone postpones retirement for financial or logistical reasons. Many people feel energetic well into their sixties and want to continue meaningful and interesting activities. They feel that retiring at sixty or sixty-five would be boring; they don't want to play golf all day, at least not yet.

As it turns out, those who want to keep going for a while may be on to something. A recent study demonstrated that early retirement may actually have "an immediate negative impact on health."[14] Of course, the statistics on death shortly after retirement are undoubtedly affected by selection bias, because some early retirees have left work due to existing health problems. But others simply have trouble finding a new reason to get out of bed, and their health deteriorates quickly as a result.

Redefining "Retirement"

As you'll see, Half-Retirement offers a solution to every one of these problems. It can help you increase the price others are willing to pay for your business, while putting you in a much better financial situation for full retirement. While nothing can guarantee the fate of your business under new leadership, Half-Retirement can offer your employees their best shot at a smooth transition.

Perhaps most importantly, Half-Retirement will disentangle you from the day-to-day demands of your business. It enables you to keep something interesting, meaningful, and profitable in your life, without wearing you out or preventing you from enjoying your

---

14   Christopher Condon, "Retiring Early Just Might Kill You, Says New Research," *Bloomberg* (December 19, 2017). Retrieved from: https://www.bloomberg.com/news/articles/2017-12-19/retiring-early-just-might-kill-you-says-new-research-eco-pulse.

hobbies and other interests. In short, you can start enjoying life more right now, instead of waiting until you're ready and able to stop working entirely.

Half-Retiring vs. Half-Retired

Half-Retirement is a way to get more free time away from your business without selling it right away. On the one hand, it's very simple: Half-Retirement just means that instead of getting rid of your business, you cut back your hours until you are working as much or as little as you'd like, while keeping your business income. However, if Half-Retirement was as simple as just working less, you would have done it already.

While the idea of Half-Retirement is very appealing to most business owners, there can be several misunderstandings about what it actually entails. Before we go any further, I want to take the time to clear up the differences between Half-Retiring and Half-Retired.

Half-Retirement is More than Just Delegation

Some business owners hear about Half-Retirement, and think, "This is great! I'll just delegate half of my work away, and then I'll be Half-Retired." Sounds reasonable, right? Pretend you had a job where you packed a hundred boxes in a typical eight-hour day, and you wanted to work four hours instead of eight. All you'd really have to do is hire someone to pack fifty boxes for you, and you'd be Half-Retired.

We have a saying around my office that it's never as simple as delegation, and it never is. Business owners don't sit around packing boxes or doing other straightforward tasks all day. On the contrary, they may wear a dozen different hats before lunch. In order to Half-Retire, you need to change the way you run your company, not just offload your work. It's not about finding someone else to pack the boxes; it's about **rethinking** the function of the box itself and questioning how it's used, when it's used, who uses it, and whether you even need it at all.

This is such a common misperception about Half-Retire, that I'm going to dwell on it a little longer. You must understand that hiring someone to help with your tasks is only a small part of the Half-Retire solution.[15] Ask yourself, are you doing a certain task because you do not want to delegate it? Of course not. Do you not know how to delegate? Of course not. Are you dying to get rid of the work? Of course, you are. The work in its current format is undelegable; that's why you have not delegated it. The sooner you accept the unpleasant reality that it's never as simple as delegating your work away, the sooner you can begin Half-Retirement. The good news is that I will show you a methodology to offload this undelegable work, so stay tuned.

Running your company involves many different skills, a profound knowledge of details, and the ability and confidence to make high-level decisions that carry far-reaching consequences. That can't be taught in a two-hour orientation session. Fortunately, Half-Retire will help you tackle these problems, one detail at a time.

Half-Retire is More than Just a Concept

On the first day of calculus class, most teachers begin by defining what calculus is. Students listen and write in their notebooks

---

15   In fact, it's actually very difficult to delegate a series of five-minute tasks. Most people are not great at constantly pivoting between helping a customer, approving a marketing campaign, double checking an invoice, and closing a sale. Research conducted at MIT confirms that successful entrepreneurs have higher than average brain dexterity, which enables them to switch more easily between the right and left sides of their brains when they are solving problems. See: Anya Kamenetz, "MIT Brain Scans Show that Entrepreneurs Really Do Think Different," *Fast Company* (January 14, 2013). Retrieved from: https://www.fastcompany.com/3004746/mit-brain-scans-show-entrepreneurs-really-do-think-different.

something like: "Calculus is the branch of mathematics that deals with the finding and properties of derivatives and integrals of functions, by methods originally based on the summation of infinitesimal differences." Maybe they even look back at their notes and memorize this definition. But does that mean they now know how to do calculus? Hardly.

Half-Retirement is more than just a concept that you learn about on an intellectual level; it is an **alternative to traditional exit planning** that takes time and deliberate planning to implement. Just because I wake up one morning and decide to be in better shape doesn't mean that I'm suddenly twenty pounds lighter and running a six-minute mile. I have to be willing to take all the incremental steps to get there: change my diet, exercise more, cut back on any bad habits I might have. In the same way, Half-Retire is just as much a lifestyle change as it is a set of ideas.

In the chapters that follow, you will learn a lot about the Half-Retire mindset, which is radically different from the way most business owners tend to think. But you cannot just switch your outlook on business instantaneously. It takes time and deliberate effort to transform the way your mind processes information and events so that you can successfully Half-Retire.

Half-Retire Won't Happen Overnight

The day you decide to Half-Retire, you are Half-Retiring. When you are drawing your current paycheck but working far less, the business-related stress is removed, and you are enjoying your time away from work, you are Half-Retired. Deciding to Half-Retire fires the starting gun. Achieving Half-Retired status is the finish line.

You couldn't just decide to sell your business today and unload it tomorrow. Between preparing financial information and positioning yourself for contract negotiations, the process could take a few months or even a few years. In the same way, transforming your business into an enterprise that you can effectively run while working only two or three days a week takes time.

It would be very easy for me to sell you a book that promises that you will only need to make a few minor adjustments in order to Half-Retire. But I'm going to be honest with you: readying your business for Half-Retirement is a process. Each step requires time and effort by you and your team, and cannot be skipped. You may need to adjust your business model, your operational model, or your personnel model. These changes may be minor and pain-less or disruptive and challenging, just like with any other kind of exit strategy.

The good news is that each step of Half-Retirement you complete brings you tangible benefits. You will have more free time. You can choose to start immediately enjoying the activities you have been missing out on all these years, or you can reinvest that time into your Half-Retirement tasks (more on this later!), thus accelerating your pace. Either way, you will get positive reinforcement along the way that will make all your efforts worth it.

CHAPTER 2

THE FUNDAMENTALS OF HALF-RETIRE

BY NOW YOU may be saying, "This Half-Retire thing sounds interesting, but how do I do it?

Half-Retirement shifts your relationship from you serving the business to it serving you. In order to make that shift, you will need to follow a system to make it happen.

Half-Retirement creates a new method to "Gracefully Exit" your business. At some point, we will all need to exit. Gracefully exiting a business, whether through Half-Retirement, selling it, or handing off to heirs, is much like selling a house. If you have ever sold a house, depending on how long you've lived there, you might need to repaint the walls, put in some new carpet, and maybe even upgrade the kitchen and bathrooms. After the inspector comes through, you may discover you have some bigger issues to address, like replacing the roof or fixing a crack in the foundation. There's nothing wrong with your house; it's just lived in.

The same goes for gracefully exiting from your business. All the idiosyncrasies in your business model—and in the systems that support it—that you've learned to live with will be exposed the moment you try to sell or exit. Some, like dirty carpet and chipped paint, are relatively quick fixes. But others, like a cracked foundation or a leaky roof, will continue to lower the value of your asset the longer you wait to address them.

Most business owners know in the back of their heads that this day of reckoning is coming, but too many just continue to work around the clock and avoid thinking about the inevitable. This is like placing buckets under the leaks in the roof when it rains: it's a "solution," but it doesn't come close to addressing the underlying issues that have to be dealt with eventually.

Half-Retirement enables you to proactively address all your business's issues long before any kind of sale or handoff. It allows you to not only fix them, but also reap the benefits from your smoothly running business (and its profits!) for many, many years. It's like being able to enjoy the granite countertops and pristine carpet while you still live in the house. Even better—unlike carpet and paint—your Half-Retirement-ready business won't wear out with use. In fact, Half-Retirement can actually cause your business to increase in value, all while you enjoy doing more of the things you love.

This chapter offers a bird's-eye view of the entire Half-Retirement process. The chapters that follow will delve into each step with a greater level of detail.

Understanding Half-Retire

"I know, Jim, I know. I need better systems so my business will run more smoothly."

That's what I hear from many owners when they first learn about Half-Retirement. Many times, they've read books, like *The E Myth*, about systematizing their business, and maybe they've even been able to apply some of the principles they learned. They know they should be working "on" the business, not "in" it, and they've made that transition with some success. But while building better systems will usually reduce some of the stress of running a business, that alone will not enable most owners to work half the time they are working now.

Half-Retirement is a completely different approach to both exit planning and creating a smoother-running business. Instead of working to create only better systems, it takes a more holistic approach with the express goal of radically reducing the owner's work time, and rethinks everything about the business from the ground up. As you can imagine, this requires some investment of time and attention on the owner's part, but the results are more than worth it.

Half-Retirement also demands that the owner adopt a completely different mindset towards their business. To Half-Retire successfully, you must transform how you think about the way you run your business and about the way you make a profit. As you'll see in the chapters that follow, the way you think about leadership and management that made you successful up to this point will most likely hinder you from successfully Half-Retiring. Transforming your mindset may feel very unnatural at first, but it is absolutely vital to getting the results you want.

Another misconception is that Half-Retirement is about delegating your work. Delegation is a component of Half-Retirement, but it's only 10 percent of the solution, not 100 percent. The remaining 90 percent is accomplished by following the Half-Retire process. After all, if getting rid of most of your work were as simple as delegation, wouldn't you have already done so? Of course. You haven't delegated your work, because it's more complex than simply delegating. We will devote significant time in this book to showing you how to break through this "can't delegate" barrier. In contrast, the Half-Retirement process may cause owners to modify or completely change their entire business, sales, and operational models. This is no small task, and many of my clients have difficulty wrapping their heads around it at first. But the great news is that these kinds of fundamental alterations make the business immensely more profitable. In fact, Half-Retirement is potentially the most profitable business move you will ever make.

What is it Like to Half-Retire?

The end result of Half-Retirement is that you will work as much as you want, doing only the work you enjoy, while still owning the business and making the high-level decisions. Hall of Fame Half-Retirees work two and a half days a week, or less, while retaining their full income. They use that extra time to finally enjoy all the things in life for which they were sacrificing at the beginning.

Not only is Half-Retirement extremely enjoyable for business owners, it also solves every major Graceful Exit impediment we covered in the last chapter. You don't have to sell your most valuable asset for pennies on the dollar. You'll stop working around the clock without dying of boredom. You will maintain your social status as an active CEO rather than a retired business owner. You'll get rid of all the tasks that annoy you, and you'll be able to offer all the great people who work for you a sense of continuity moving forward.

As I've mentioned, Half-Retirement is not something I dreamed up all on my own. It started when I was fourteen years old working at my grandfather's company. Grandpa had passed away and his brother was now the CEO of the company. I witnessed him take off four solid months every winter to golf in Boca Raton. The company continued to run like a Swiss watch, even though Rudy was gone. I nicknamed this ideal scenario "The Uncle Rudy Plan," and hoped to achieve the same status some day.

Contrast this with the thousands of businesses I have worked with since then. They skipped vacations or stressed when they did. Why could they not achieve Uncle Rudy status? Because they were approaching their businesses with the wrong intent. No one starts a business with the goal to work a couple of half-days a week, right? We are willing to work hard, and we build the processes, business model, management systems, and everything else to work under that premise. That methodology continues until you are ready to exit. It's a freight train rumbling down the tracks with great inertia.

The Half-Retire process changes the direction of that freight train's inertia through a comprehensive solution that shifts all your business's resources to serve your retirement.

Half-Retire is a comprehensive solution that emerged from thousands of hours of helping business owners address all these problems individually. This means that the system has benefited from the tremendous wisdom and experiences of some of the most successful entrepreneurs in the country.

Half-Retirement is about breaking the habits you formed while launching your business that no longer serve you well. Getting a business off the ground involves a lot of experimentation and often a lot of crisis management as well. You put out the fires and go with what works, because that's what enables you to keep going, not because you've determined beyond a shadow of a doubt that the way you do it necessarily works best.

Half-Retirement helps you move beyond just running your business in a way that works, to running it in the most efficient and effective way possible. We do this by leveraging business model innovation, process redesign, and technology that even non-techie people can use easily. Again, this is completely different from writing out a list of tasks you perform and getting someone else to do them for you. This is changing the fundamental way your company functions.

What does this kind of radical redesign look like? In the chapters that follow, you'll read about many examples of business owners like you who have successfully made the transition. But the corporate world also offers both successful and unsuccessful examples. Larger corporations often have to make radical adjustments when new technology, market changes, and all sorts of external disruptions render a previously successful business model obsolete. One of the starkest examples is the advent of the digital camera, which destroyed the business models of many large camera companies that relied on selling film at a huge margin.

Kodak—which dominated the marketplace for decades—was ultimately unable to adjust successfully and filed for bankruptcy in 2012. By contrast, Fujifilm radically altered the way it made money, investing heavily in training its internal experts in new digital technology. Today, it still sells cameras, but other sectors, like its medical imaging equipment, are growing rapidly as well. It has also successfully leveraged its expertise in chemicals (from the days of film) for entirely different industries, such as cosmetics.[16]

Kodak and Fujifilm began with similar business models and products, with Kodak being the dominant player. The difference was that Fujifilm's leadership was willing to invest the time, effort, and money to successfully transition to a digital world, while Kodak's leadership tried to keep its existing business model on life support, tweaking it here and there. In the same way, whether or not you can make the successful transition to Half-Retirement depends on your willingness to follow through on the necessary changes you decide to make.

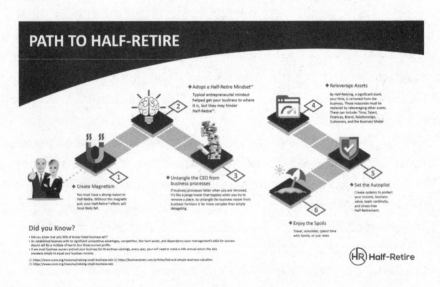

PATH TO HALF-RETIRE

---

16   K.N.C., "Sharper Focus: The History of the Rivalry Between Fujifilm and Kodak is More Relevant than Ever," *Economist* (January 18, 2012). Retrieved from: https://www.economist.com/schumpeter/2012/01/18/sharper-focus.

The Six Steps to Half-Retirement

Transforming your business from the ground up may sound like an intimidating process, but in reality, there are just six basic steps you will need to complete in order to successfully Half-Retire. We will cover each in extensive detail in the following chapters. For now, here is a brief overview:

1. **Create Magnetism**

You must have a strong reason to Half-Retire, and you must be constantly aware of that reason. We call this creating a "magnet" to pull you toward Half-Retirement. Half-Retirement requires a lot more than willpower to execute successfully. If you do not have a strong pull from your magnet, the Half-Retirement process will just feel like a lot of extra work.

2. **Adopt a Half-Retire Mindset**

As we've discussed already, the mindset that has made your business successful so far will most likely hinder your ability to Half-Retire. You must change how you think about your business as well as how you make money from your business in order to radically reduce your hours while keeping your income.

3. **Untangle the CEO (You!) from the Business Processes**

Most business owners are involved in nearly every aspect of their business, from sales and customer service, to production and fulfillment. You may feel like it is impossible to disentangle yourself from the day-to-day workings of your business, but don't worry. The Half-Retire system will help you tackle this, one step and one detail at a time.

4. **Re-leverage Assets**

During Half-Retirement, we will be removing a valuable asset from the business—you! The easiest way to replace that lost asset is to re-leverage other assets in the business. Every business has under-leveraged assets. These can include time, human capital, finances, brand strength, industry relationships, customer networks, and the business model itself. Fujifilm didn't know that the nanotechnology it used to apply chemicals to film could revolutionize the cosmetics industry until its leaders took the time to scour the company for underleveraged assets. During the fourth step of Half-Retirement, you'll learn to identify these within your company and leverage them to your advantage.

5. **Protect Your Progress**

Once you untangle yourself from the day-to-day processes and determine your underleveraged assets, you will be ready to create Half-Retirement systems to protect them. Specifically, these systems will protect your income, the value of your business, and team continuity. Ultimately, step five is what enables you to have a stress-free Half-Retirement.

6. **Enjoy Your New Life**

Once you've completed the first five steps, your job is to enjoy your Half-Retirement. Live the life that you've always wanted, before you're too old to enjoy it. Start relaxing, taking time for your hobbies, traveling, and spending time with friends and family, all while keeping your income and the work that you like most.

Bob's Story

Anyone who has sold a house understands that fair market value for the house is the price that someone is willing to pay. That's why you could have a beautiful seven-bedroom colonial in the suburbs of Dallas go for the same price as a run-down efficiency in New York City. It doesn't matter how many memories you have in the house or what you think it's worth. The house will sell for what a buyer is willing to bring to closing.

Unfortunately, many business owners forget this basic lesson when it comes to selling their company. They look at the price they need to meet their financial planning needs and waste countless weeks, months, or even years preparing (and hoping) for a sale that's never going to happen.

A friend of mine, whom I'll call "Bob," owns a great company that has given him an enviable income for many years. He lives in his dream house, sends his kids to private school, and generally enjoys the lifestyle he wants. But like all of us, he's not getting any younger. So, he went to his financial planner to find out how much money he needed in order to retire comfortably. Then he came to see me.

The number Bob's financial planner gave him was about five times what his business paid him annually, so that's the number he used to determine his selling price. On the one hand, I could understand why he thought he might be able to sell for that number. His business model was sound, and his profit margins and market share would make his company attractive to buyers. Despite these attractive aspects, I told him that I thought most buyers would be willing to pay him three times his annual profits, or possibly four at the most.

"Are you sure?" Bob asked, sounding deflated. I assured him I was. He told me he absolutely had to get five times his annual earnings or he couldn't afford to retire. But he was really getting tired of doing sales work and other tasks that drained a lot of his physical and mental energy. So, he hired a broker, paid several thousand dollars for an appraisal, and hoped his healthy profits and solid niche market would magically give him the sale price he needed.

After months of preparing documents, meetings, and marketing the business for the sale, an offer finally came in. And it was exactly what I had told him it would be, right around three times his annual earnings. Rather than view the offer from this experienced buyer as "fair," Bob said, "No thanks," and looked for more buyer prospects. After a year of entertaining additional offers and spending hundreds of hours negotiating, preparing data, and dreaming of his big check, Bob gave up. All the offers came in around three times his annual earnings, not the five times the earnings Bob needed.

Like so many business owners, Bob "backed into" the sale price for his business, asking for what he wanted and hoping for the best, instead of recognizing what it would be worth to buyers. Simply put, prospective buyers didn't care what Bob needed to get out of the business. They cared about what they could reasonably expect to get out of it.

Instead of spending time pursuing a fantasy deal that was never going to happen—while still working long days running his business—Bob could have spent those two years Half-Retired. He could have stopped doing the sales work he didn't like anymore, enjoyed his life, and kept his income stream. He might have discovered that he could live happily like that for another ten years, or he might still have been ready to find a buyer.

Either way, when Half-Retired Bob was ready to sell, he would have gotten at least the same price that he ended up getting by exiting the traditional way. But he would have saved time and energy, made money, and enjoyed life more in the process.

I always tell clients who are ready to retire: if you can be happy taking the sale price that someone is willing to pay for your business right now, go ahead and sell! That is a Graceful Exit. There's no point continuing to run your business if you don't want to, if you are satisfied with the price you can get. But if you don't want to take that price, consider Half-Retirement!

Allison's Story

Sometimes getting the right price for the business isn't a problem. A client of mine, "Allison," was interested in selling her software company. She was in her mid-sixties, and although she loved her work, she was definitely ready to slow down and spend more time with her grandchildren while they were still young.

Fortunately, Allison's business was very attractive to buyers, because it had a lot of recurring revenue due to long-term contracts with big customers. These customers not only bought in huge volume, but they were also very satisfied with her product and the support services she offered.

For all of these reasons, Allison would have had no problem getting the price she wanted under normal circumstances. However, she had a huge number of conditions that she wanted to attach to the sale. Allison loved her employees and did not want any staffing changes made by whoever bought her company. This spoke very highly of her as a person and a business leader, but it simply wasn't realistic to expect a new owner to make all of the same personnel decisions she had made. All of the non-financial terms Allison wanted to attach to the sale made a deal undoable.

Half-Retirement is a perfect solution for someone like Allison, because she can continue to make all the leadership and staffing decisions in the company without getting bogged down in the day-to-day operations. By Half-Retiring, business owners like Allison can still call the shots, while relaxing and enjoying the rest of their lives in the process.

Four Types of Half-Retirees

Okay, you've decided to Half-Retire. You understand it may involve a radical transformation of the way you do business, but you're okay with that because it creates the door to a Graceful Exit you've been looking for. You're ready to get started and make those changes.

I want to make sure that it's all smooth sailing from here on out, but there are several ways you can get off track. I want to make sure we don't start our journey on the wrong foot. After observing thousands of business owners make this transition, I've noticed four major patterns of behavior:

The Dreamer

The Dreamer wants to Half-Retire in theory but just can't seem to get it done in practice. Typical Dreamers get really excited when they first learn about the system and start imagining all the things they'll do with their newfound free time. Check in with them two years later, however, and they still have not made any significant progress toward their goals.

Many business owners are visionaries and have no trouble grasping the concept of Half-Retirement. However, Dreamers find the daily pull of their business too strong to overcome. They want the end results of Half-Retirement, but they struggle with the little choices they must make every day to prioritize the process.

There is a big difference between Half-Retiring and Half-Retired. Being Half-Retired means you have successfully transformed your business into an equity income-producing asset that requires only minimal work from you. Half-Retiring is the process you go through to *get to* Half-Retired status. Dreamers are perpetually Half-Retiring but never make it to Half-Retired status.

Connie: A Dreamer in Action

Connie's twenty-five-year-old company supplied office furniture, and she was the perfect candidate for Half-Retirement. She knew she wasn't in a position to sell her company, because she still needed more income than a sale could provide. After learning about the

Half-Retire system, she loved the concept and said, "I'm going to do this." She took our free initial course, and she fully understood that the process was more in-depth than just hiring a manager so she could spend more time away from the office.

"I know I need to do this," she assured me. "I'm going to get it done."

Since she didn't opt for coaching or our training program, I wished Connie well and followed up with her six months later, just to see how things were going. I asked about a couple of milestones on the Half-Retire list.

"Well, we had a problem with one of our suppliers last month, and then we had to onboard a few new customers," she explained. The longer she went on, the clearer it became that she felt she was too busy running her company to make any progress towards Half-Retirement. But she promised me she would do better.

Our next phone call (another six months later) yielded the same types of excuses. Connie was a classic Dreamer. She truly believed she was too busy to get through even the most basic steps of Half-Retirement, and as the months went by, it was becoming clear that it was never really going to happen.

Meanwhile, nothing had changed about the conditions that had led Connie to say, "I need to do this." She still did! However, the longer she waited, the greater the chance became that she would never be able to retire in a meaningful way at all.

Half-Retirement can be accomplished in a reasonable time frame with an investment of as little as a few hours a week. But business owners must make it a priority, and for some, this may require some accountability. Dreamers like Connie need to shift their mindset, and have a greater sense of urgency, which they are sometimes unable to create on their own.

The Turtle

Turtles decide to Half-Retire, and they mean it. Often, they take immediate action. They may even make significant strides early in the process, especially with the low-hanging fruit.

However, they fail to leverage these successes into meaningful progress. They put in an hour here and an hour there. These hours eventually add up to Half-Retirement, but a few hours a month does not create enough momentum to fully benefit from Half-Retirement. The turtle-like pace yields some good things for the owner, but leaves the bulk of the benefits unseized. Now, I want to be clear that there isn't one set pace for the ideal Half-Retirement. The length of time it takes to go from working full time to working only two or three days a week will depend on all sorts of factors. These include the state of the company, the level of cooperation and buy-in from the employees, and how much time the owner is willing and able to invest each week.

The entire process of Half-Retirement can take a fully committed owner anywhere from a few months to a few years. As a general rule, though, you should be able to make significant progress toward Half-Retirement in a few months. But if you don't regularly make at least some time for it, it won't happen at all.

The Jack Rabbit

As you might expect, where the Turtle moves too slowly, the Jack Rabbit is off to the races. Jack Rabbits love the idea of Half-Retirement, and they often employ lots of good people they trust. This is the ideal situation for Jack Rabbits. They create the game plan to reprocess their work through the Half-Retirement system, but they skip three of the four steps, jumping straight to the part where they get rid of their work. After all, the team is very talented and can handle more advanced tasks, so why not?

The problem is that while the Jack Rabbits think they are Half-Retiring, they're really just delegating (or abdicating) in disguise. By week two, they've already left the building for an extended vacation. But when they finally make it back, they're in for a rude awakening.

Half-Retirement is a process. You start out with a long weekend once a month. Then you get a real vacation. After a while, you're only coming in two days a week. The Half-Retire Plan works if you follow it. To do that, you absolutely cannot skip steps.

The World Traveler

World Travelers have that magical combination of both urgency and patience. They follow the Half-Retire process, avoiding the temptations of staying theoretical, going too slowly, or rushing through the list. The rewards for their stellar execution are many. They enjoy a stable income, plenty of stress-free time off, and a happy staff, all while retaining the immensely valuable asset they have spent so many years building.

Become a World Traveler

Although business owners can become Dreamers, Turtles, and Jack Rabbits based on their personalities and propensities, I can assure you that anyone can become a World Traveler. If you follow the principles and procedures outlined in the chapters that follow, you will develop the skills and systems you need to Half-Retire successfully.

Half-Retirement is a revolutionary yet realistic solution to exit planning. Instead of waiting and wasting time (while your retirement worries grow), Half-Retirement will enable you to take charge today and create your Graceful Exit.

CHAPTER 3

THE UNSELLABLE BUSINESS

"**THIS GUY JUST** Sold His Business for $50 Million!"

We've all seen those headlines and imagined what it would be like to get a payday like that, ditch all the headaches, and ride off into the sunset. Such examples of extraordinary success can be inspiring, but they can also create completely unrealistic expectations for the valuation and sale of most businesses.

Behind the clickbait, there's always more to the story. For example, if the company in question was either publicly traded or funded by venture capitalists, the original owners are getting a nice payday, but they're not usually walking away with the entire pile of cash. Furthermore, for a company to sell for a "never have to work again" number, there are usually seven figures of profits or some secret sauce. These could include a new and exciting business model with no competition, a technological edge or patent, an invaluable brand, or something else that most of us don't have. I've never been in that situation, and I'm guessing you haven't either.

For most of us considering the sale of our businesses, the potential pot of gold at the end of the rainbow isn't as big as it needs to be. In fact, the pot of gold may be more like a bucket or may be empty. According to the International Business Brokers Association, up to 90 percent of business listings will not be purchased by anyone.[17]

---

17   Richard Parker, "The Business For Sale Marketplace – Why 90% Of Listings Never Sell," Forbes (October 24, 2016). Retrieved from: https://www.forbes.com/sites/richardparker/2016/10/24/the-business-for-sale-marketplace-why-90-of-listings-never-sell/#319c3e2216d8.

If you're already excited about Half-Retiring instead of selling the business soon, please feel free to skim or skip this chapter and move on to the next section. But I have found that many business owners can see the potential benefits of Half-Retirement while staying on the fence about whether to sell instead. This chapter will help you think through that decision and explore some of the most common roadblocks to a good sale price.

Good Reasons to Sell Your Business

Although this book focuses on the process and benefits of Half-Retirement, I want to reiterate that there can be many good reasons to sell your business. The first, and most important, is that you are happy with a sale price you have been offered by an actual buyer. I meet plenty of business owners whose enterprises are ready to sell with minimal preparation and adjustments. As I mentioned in the last chapter, if you have a realistic expectation of sales price and it creates a Graceful Exit, then you should probably sell the business.

Other sound reasons to sell include changes in the market, industry, or economy that give you good cause to believe your business will become significantly less profitable in the near future. Let's say you owned a video-rental store in the early 2000s, before streaming services became ubiquitous. If you understood that internet speeds were only going to get faster, that would have been a great time to sell. Think of it like musical chairs. Your market insight may alert you that the music is about to stop; selling gives you a chance to grab a chair before that happens.

Of course, no one knows the future with absolute precision and accuracy, so it can be difficult to determine the ideal time to get out. Until a particular disruption actually occurs—no matter how inevitable it is—there will still be money to be made. Video stores were profitable until they weren't. We all know driverless cars are coming, but do truck drivers have another five profitable years or another thirty? It's hard to say. The best we can do is become expert observers in our industry and take our best guesses.

There are also plenty of personal reasons that can make selling your business the most sensible decision. Maybe you're starting a new business and don't want to be bothered with running two at once. Maybe you're moving to a different city and your business is strictly local. If running your business remotely after the move is more trouble than it's worth, then selling makes sense.

There are countless changes in life that can affect running your business. These include kids growing up and leaving home, a health challenge, a partnership gone wrong, and the loss of a spouse. Some owners become bored with their businesses or lose their passion for what they are doing. They may feel like they are no longer learning and growing in their role, and they are ready to try something new. All of those are perfectly good reasons to sell.

And of course, sometimes owners have profited so well from their years of running their business that they really don't need any more money. They want to pass on the business to an heir—a child, a mentee, or an employee—letting someone new take the reins and enjoy the profits. This, too, is a Graceful Exit.

Common Obstacles to Selling

Selling a business—even a highly desirable one—is a long, complicated process. There is simply no way around this unpleasant reality. Even if a serious and qualified buyer comes to the table right away, the sale will likely take six to twelve months. Obviously, if you have any trouble stirring up interest, the process can take years.

But how do you know if your business is even sellable at all? To answer this question, you have to switch your thinking from that of a seller to that of a buyer. This means you have to stop focusing on what you need to get out of the sale and put yourself in the buyer's shoes. For buyers, determining the purchase price is all about assessing the risk and determining if your winning formula will work for them. For them to see clearly that purchasing your business is likely to have a better risk-reward ratio than other investment options, they have to be reasonably sure they can run it successfully.

Buyers want to know what your business has already achieved, not what it *could have* achieved if this or that had gone differently. They are going to be willing to pay for demonstrated sales volume and profitability, not unrealized potential. I've had many potential sellers object to this, saying "Jim! All the new owner has to do is make a couple of adjustments, and he'll be making three times the profit I'm making." Let's say for the sake of argument that this is 100 percent true, and there really are a few changes that could greatly increase your profitability. You just haven't gotten around to making them, because you know you're on your way out. The buyer is going to ask himself, "If this change is such a goldmine, why hasn't the owner already done it?" The most logical explanation is that the idea isn't worth implementing for a reason, and that reason is a good one. All this is why—even if you are selling for the right reasons—you may encounter obstacles.

There are countless reasons that a business may be difficult to sell, but in my experience, most of these reasons fall into one of two categories: conflict between the buyer and the seller over the assignment of risk, and the inability to disentangle the owner from the day-to-day operations of the business.

Assignment of Risk

Buying any business involves a degree of risk—even if that business is immensely profitable—and no buyer is willing to assume risk for free. Trying to push risk onto sellers without compensating them for it, either with a lower price or better terms such as an earn-out payment system, will ruin the sale every time. Of course, once in a blue moon, a buyer will overpay for a business. We've all heard the stories of Old Bob who sold for millions when he was about to give up and shut down the business. I don't recommend betting on this "win the lottery" retirement scenario. When you are the one selling, you need to assume that the buyer will figure out a way to accurately assess each and every risk associated with your business, so you should, too.

The unpleasant truth is that most of the risks of transferring a business are best assessed and controlled by the seller. Whichever party can assess and/or control risks is in the best position to take any particular risk. In the case of a business sale, the seller has much better knowledge and control of risks, while the buyer is in the dark. However, I encounter many sellers who see a business sale as a way to push all of their unwanted headaches and risks onto some unwitting buyer. Buyers aren't stupid. They will identify all the risks and rightly ask you to assume the appropriate ones or compensate them for "insuring" the risk.

This is where deals blow up. The seller wants to wash his hands of the business and any issues, but the buyer wants to minimize his risk. These desires are opposed to one another. Unless these opposing risks can be balanced, there will be no sale. For deals to get done, the seller usually comes to the buyer, not vice versa. It's perfectly reasonable for the buyer to worry about customer and employee continuity or skeletons in the closet. These are real risks, and if the seller wants to push those risks onto the buyer, there will need to be some compensation.

To understand how a prospective buyer will view your business, you will need to think realistically about many different kinds of risk. Here are a few of the major categories:

1. Disruption

    - Human beings naturally resist change to something that has been working for them. Sure, we don't mind Starbucks offering red cups around the holidays or our doctor's office installing new carpet in the waiting room. But we usually don't like it when our favorite restaurant radically changes the menu or when the beloved principal at our kids' school retires.

- In the same way, successful businesses thrive on continuity. Customers and employees—as long as they are reasonably happy—prefer knowing that everything is going to be the same tomorrow as it was yesterday. This continuity is always at risk of disruption during and after a sale. A change of ownership will "wake up" slightly dissatisfied customers and employees and nudge them to reconsider quitting. Some will quit. Buyers know this is a real risk and will typically mitigate it with attractive terms or discounts to the purchase price.

2. Detractors

- Buyers are going to be alert for any hidden risks or "skeletons in the closet" associated with your business. Don't take this the wrong way. Every business has issues that are not a big deal to you but will be a big deal to someone new. Maybe your books are audited or in pristine condition, and you've been showing healthy profits for ten years. But then they notice that a huge portion of your volume comes from a single customer. They're going to want assurance that that customer isn't about to leave, and it may be difficult for you to prove it without tipping off the customer about your intent to sell.

- Maybe you run the most popular hardware store in a small town, but you heard a rumor that Home Depot is planning to open a new store a mile away. A new competitor of that magnitude would seriously affect your business's profitability heading into the future. Any sensible buyer will do due diligence and investigate these kinds of possibilities.

3. Changes in the Big Picture

    ▪ If you are selling because you think certain market, technological, or economic changes on the horizon will lower your revenues, realize that your potential buyers may be aware of those factors, too. They might have a new business model or approach in mind to mitigate those changes, but again, they're not going to pay you for any innovations they plan to make on their own.

4. Unrealistic Terms and Conditions

    ▪ Remember the software company owner in the last chapter? She wanted the buyers to promise to keep all her staff for as long as they wanted to work there. Any invasive conditions like these will present potential obstacles to a sale. (Of course, some buyers may sign your contract and then ignore your wishes, since they are typically unenforceable.)

    ▪ Other unrealistic terms include:

        * Receiving 100 percent of the sale price upfront.

        * Being unwilling to work in the business after sale. I understand that you just want to be

done with it when you sell, but that greatly increases the risk for the buyer.

* Expecting the buyer to trust off-the-books transactions. Buyers will base their purchase on tax records. It is unlikely you will receive credit for unrecorded cash receipts or other off-the-books transactions.

* Guaranteeing jobs for any employee.

* Keeping your company-paid perks. Yes, people ask for this.

Nothing Works without You

When you go shopping for clothes, you don't just look for style and functionality; you look for the right size. The highest quality clothes at the best price are not worth anything to you if you can't wear them. In the same way, the most profitable business in the world may be worth nothing to buyers if they can't run it without you.

There are several ways in which an owner may become completely entangled with the essential processes of the business. These are realities that most people don't give any thought to until it's time to sell.

1. Everyone depends on your expertise or "magic touch."

   - If you are the only one in the business who knows how to think strategically, close the big sales, or solve certain problems, then you will have a hard time removing yourself from the day-to-day workings of the business so a new owner can take over easily. (This is also a key reason that you probably find it difficult to take extended time off.)

Executive-level talent is notoriously difficult and expensive to replace, and your buyers know this. Plus, the buyer is worried that no one but you can do this. If you are Picasso, you can't substitute another painter.

2.   Every process and decision involves you.

- There are many reasons why the business won't work if you're not there. It could be your unique skill set (see Item 1), or it could be that your physical presence causes people to behave differently than they do when you are away. Maybe you are the primary decisionmaker at every level, so your employees can only move the ball forward so far in any process without consulting you directly. If you are an important gear in the machine, removing that gear will cause the machine to stop. Whatever the reason, if your business doesn't run smoothly without you there, then you are going to have a lot of trouble selling it to someone else.

3.   Your employees only want to work for you.

- Being a beloved boss can have a downside. "Stan" owns a convenience store with two loyal employees: Mary, a middle-aged woman who has worked for him since she was a teenager, and his nephew who comes in and helps out after school.

- As Stan got older, Mary started doing more and more around the store, taking care of bank drops and stocking shelves without complaint. Stan's nephew is great with computers and maintains all the inventory and accounting systems.

- Both Mary and Stan's nephew add a lot of value to Stan's business, and they do it because of their personal connection to him. Would they be willing to do the same for a new owner? Possibly, but that's far from guaranteed. This isn't an insurmountable obstacle to a sale, but it is a factor that any buyer will consider seriously.

4. The customers only want to deal with you.

- One of the most serious obstacles to the sale of an otherwise sound business is when the customers—the lifeblood of the business—only want to deal with the owner.

- There can be a variety of reasons for this. In some cases, like the employees in the previous example, the owner has cultivated personal relationships with his customers, and they choose to patronize his business over others because of that relationship.

- The owner may also be the face of the business, handling the majority (or all!) of the sales and customer service, while the employees handle only unseen support tasks. This may make for a profitable business (and a busy owner), but it is not a business that another person could easily take over.

Why I Sold my Auto-Repair Shops

Remember the auto-repair franchises I bought during law school? Those stores ran well and made money. But I was still in my twenties, so I hadn't yet figured out how to get them to run well without me there.

I sold them for a combination of reasons, most of them good. I knew that the advent of aluminized exhaust systems was going to present a technological disruption to the industry that was going to mess up our business model. This was a fixable problem, but I didn't want to be the one to deal with it. I was also tired of running the stores and preparing to start a new business. So, I sold the stores for three times their annual profit and got out.

Selling under these conditions was a totally defensible decision. But knowing what I know now, I would have fixed the business model and my systems and Half-Retired, even in my twenties.

Why I Shouldn't Have Sold my Auto-Repair Shops

It's a good thing I was twenty-seven when I sold my shops. I had the luxury to give up my hard and unpaid work building a good income stream, because I wanted to move on. An older and wiser version of myself realizes that the better move might have been to Half-Retire at twenty-seven.

When you start a business, you work long and sometimes unpaid hours. I know I did. You are building value in the business with this value-add. However, you cannot extract this value from the business until much later.

As the business matures, your long hours subside and you can begin to pay yourself fair value for your services. At some point, you have built a strong-enough foundation to allow you to extract *more* value than you are giving. This isn't overcompensation; It's making up for all that underpaid work you did early on.

Right when I was hitting the inflection point, I sold the business and let the buyer extract all that value I had created early on. There's no need for you to make the same mistake.

Evaluating Your Business

When we're thinking of selling, we need to think of all the options a buyer can choose. Yes, buying a business yields a significant income stream, but so does an annuity, insurance policy, stocks, and real estate. These investments are sources of passive income. They offer a consistent payout to its owner, who doesn't have to do anything except receive it. In contrast, buying even a well-run business is much closer to buying an annuity that comes with a job. Ask yourself, is buying your business a better deal than buying a passive investment that has no job-related headaches?

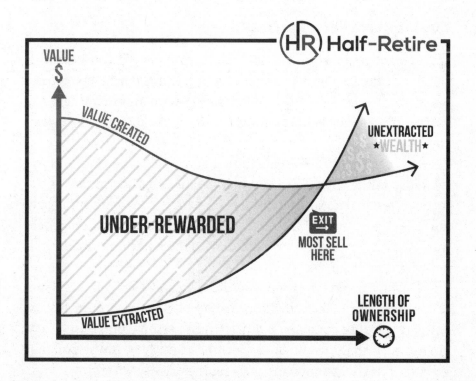

This doesn't mean that a new owner doesn't expect to do any work at all. Doctors buying medical practices from other doctors expect to work, but they do not expect to pay much for the "job" part of the business. In purchasing the practice, they are buying an established network of patients and a reputation in the community. They may also be buying real estate, equipment, furniture, and systems for processes like billing and record keeping. They do not pay the other doctor for the privilege of being a doctor. They already paid their medical school and training hospitals for that, both in money and in years of labor.

Yet when we evaluate our own businesses, we lose this sense of perspective. We tend to underestimate how much of our profits are generated by our own labor and overestimate how much is generated by "the business." To get a more accurate picture of our business, we need to consider the following factors:

The Limits of Personal Brand

Lots of small and medium-sized businesses enjoy great success with personal branding, especially at the beginning. An owner-centric business often leads to greater profitability, even over many decades, because the owner is doing much of the work directly, instead of paying employees.

However, focusing too much on a personal brand can limit the salability of the company. I was told by an employee of one of the top motivational speakers that the company's sales were cut nearly ten times when the owner passed away. It turns out that most people wanted to deal only with the person with the name on the door and not with other trainers.

A strong personal brand may have made your company successful and profitable; however, it may also make it hard to sell. Retreating from a company built around a personal brand isn't easy, but it can be done. Just do not expect the buyer to be the person that executes this tricky move and pays for the privilege of trying.

Enterprise Value vs. Profitability

For most businesses, the fair market price for the business is related to profitability, as opposed to its intangible value. Many business owners see gems in their assets and want the sale price to reflect them. These gems might include patents or pending patents, trademarks, special equipment, business processes, trade secrets, brands, marquis customers, or any other valued asset.

Business owners expect buyers to see the value of these gems the same way they do. Buyers typically do not. Here's why: if the gems are so valuable, they should be yielding profit and already reflected in your sales price.

Sometimes a strategic buyer can take your assets and deploy them differently and more profitably than you. When this is the case, you can receive additional compensation for these assets. For instance, a consumer goods producer ran a break-even business. However, he had a strong brand and good selling margin. By closing his factory and consolidating production, the buyer was able to turn a break-even business into nearly $1 million of annual profit. The seller can get paid some of the upside in these types of situations. However, if you cannot demonstrate a clear path to extract new value from your hidden gems, do not expect them to be reflected in the sales price.

Business Model Evaluation

I have written an entire book on business models,[18] so I will do my best to summarize 360 pages in one. Your business model has three components: your offer to your customers, how you monetize that offering, and how you sustain that monetization. To evaluate your offering, consider your products or services, and your target market. Is your offering targeted at an attractive market? Do you have the right value proposition? How does your offer compare to competitors?

---

18   See: Jim Muehlhausen, *Business Models for Dummies* (Hoboken: John Wiley & Sons, Inc., 2013).

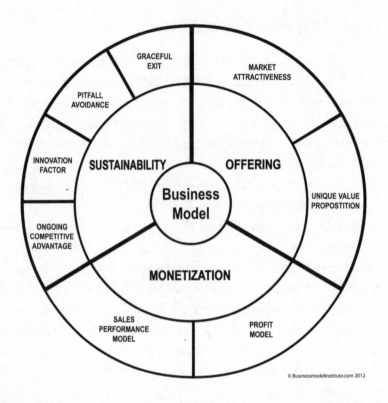

© Businessmodelinstitute.com 2012

To evaluate your monetization, consider both your profitability and your sales performance. Is the model by which you make profit better or worse than competitors? (Think eBay versus Amazon. Both sell similar items on the internet, but they have very different profit models.) How does your sales and marketing team execute? Think of IBM in the 1970s and 1980s. Most experts felt that other brands were superior in performance to IBM, but IBM was vastly superior at executing the sales strategy. Evaluating the sustainability of your business model is key to whether or not you can sell for a desirable price. Questions to ask yourself include: is your competitive advantage going to last? How likely are you to out-innovate competitors or be out-innovated? What other pitfalls lie on the horizon? These are the questions that buyers will be asking about your business, so you are much better off asking them of yourself first, before you try to sell.

Systems Evaluation

Even if your business model is fully sustainable, you will need to evaluate your systems to determine if they are easily transferable to another owner. In a perfect world, the buyer would love to see that you have formalized systems and processes. In the real world, business owners have very little in the way of documented systems. The buyer will be sure to check out the systems in place for all your processes, including marketing, sales, recruiting, hiring, training, accounting, payroll, purchasing, production, inventory management, fulfillment, collection, and customer service. The better the system and its documentation, the more easily someone else can step into your role, and the more your systems add value to your enterprise.

Pay special attention to things like software. Often, we develop a patchwork of software packages and physical records that works fine for us, because we know exactly where everything is, which makes it challenging for someone else to step in and take over. The new owner will want everything to be streamlined and efficient. A patchwork of electronic systems will not kill a deal, but it may lower your sales price as the buyer budgets part of what used to be your sales price to purchase the software you should have in place but don't.

The Acid Test

Business valuation can be a very useful tool, but it is not cheap. Once you go through the process and get the estimated value, you're not any closer to being ready for the sale. Here's why: it's an estimate. The evaluators aren't offering to buy your business. They are guessing what someone should pay. Most valuations are based heavily on financial data. That means they do not take into account the detractors we just discussed; they just run the numbers. Buyers, however, do take other factors into account. So, many sales do not get done for the valuation estimate.

Here is an approximate but quick and low-cost way to get a ballpark valuation:

1. Use an online calculator to get a rough estimate for the sales price of your business

2. Assume for the sake of argument that the business will sell for that and only that

3. Assume you will get 25 percent upfront and 25 percent per year for three additional years

4. Assume you will lose 5 to 10 percent for charge-offs and other issues

This is not a precise measurement, of course, but it will get you in the ballpark of what you are likely to receive. If this number is close to what you need or hope to get, then it may make sense to proceed with preparing your business for sale. If it's not, you may need to look at other options, such as Half-Retirement. For a more accurate measurement of what your business will sell for, always consult a trusted broker or accountant.

Reality Check

So, what happens when real business owners sell? I'll give you three quick examples. When I sold my auto-repair franchise, the first deal I had fell through at the very last minute over a tiny detail. I had already endorsed a large check, assuming the deal was done. It doesn't get much closer to "done" than a signed contract and a signed check, right? Instead of moving on to the next business I had already started, I had to jump right back into work and start the sales process over while running both businesses. The second deal

I got wasn't nearly as good as the first, but I took it anyway, because I had mentally checked out of the business. It took me nine years to get my earn-out, and even then, I had to sue the buyer for it.

A client of mine, "Kyle," was completely ready to be done with his business. It was earning Kyle $450,000 annually, but had one customer account for 80 percent of the sales. I was able to find only one buyer willing to take the customer exit risk, and he was willing to pay only $1.1 million (only 2.4 times earnings). But the sale was contingent upon Kyle's willingness to stick around for at least two years, because the company couldn't survive without his relationships. Kyle really didn't want to do this, and the deal nearly blew up over him staying engaged. Once he realized this term was a deal breaker, he reluctantly agreed, because it was the only way to get his money. As of this writing, he is getting ready to renew his employment contract for another two years, because he has found that he doesn't mind working so much when he doesn't have to deal with the headaches of being the owner.

Another client, "Tony," built an engineering sales company that paid him between $500,000 and $1 million in his worst years and $4 million in his best. Yet the best offer he got for the company was $6.8 million (1.7 times the average audited profit over the past two years). Plus, the terms contained a clause that required him to stay on as a salesman for two years. But Tony really wanted to "just be done" with the business, so he took it.

Remember, these three examples represent part of that 10 percent of businesses that actually sell, so these are success stories. In most cases, the annual payout from a sale isn't much more than what you would receive by Half-Retiring, except that, while your payout from selling the business ends, Half-Retirement income continues.

Preparing Your Business for Sale

Once you decide to sell, there are several important steps to give your sale the best chance of success. Many books explain in great detail how to sell your business, so I will offer a brief overview of the process here.

1. Prepare the last two years of credible financial records.

    - Whether or not you use an agent or broker, potential buyers will need to see clear records of income and expenditures, as well as proof that you are paying your taxes and complying with all applicable laws and regulations. You will need to adjust your salary to fair market value, remove any personal expenses from the books, and report any cash transactions that are off the books. Audited financials are best as it eliminates uncertainty for the buyer. Expect to pay $5,000–$10,000 for each year's audit.

2. Create a buyer's book.

    - While smaller businesses don't necessarily need to bother with this step, any business selling for seven figures or more is better off with a buyer's book. This is a basic marketing tool to give to potential buyers, like the online description and photographs of a house. It should describe the history of the company, the financial picture, the staff, and the business model. These books generally cost between $5,000 and $20,000 to produce.

3. Secure key employees.

- Through a combination of one-on-one meetings and contract negotiations, you need to ensure that all your key employees are committed to continue under new ownership. Don't try to avoid this step by hoping that no one will notice you are selling. They will find out eventually, so make sure you give them what they will need to work happily for a new owner.

4. Secure key customers.

- You will also need to communicate with your key customers to ensure that they will continue to do business with the new owners. Review pricing, customer service, and all the other relevant factors to make sure the new owners will be able to keep them just as happy as you have.

5. Remove detractors.

- Check for all those skeletons in the closet that we discussed in the earlier section and get rid of them.

6. Make sure your business model is transferable.

- You will need to eliminate any dependence of the business model on you and your direct involvement. You may need to adjust the way you make money to ensure that someone else can make money from the company after a sale. We will discuss this process in greater detail in the chapters that follow.

7. Make sure your systems are transferable.

   - You will also need to adjust all your systems so that someone else can step into your role with ease. This means standardizing them—so everyone knows what's expected and required—and carefully documenting them.

8. Remember that the only valuation that matters is what the buyer will pay and can afford to pay. For most small business deals, this translates to what the Small Business Administration (SBA) will finance.

   - You can get any number of professional valuations, but since most purchases are financed with Small Business Administration loans, their process is the only one that matters in the end.

While some sellers attend meticulously to all these details, most do not. They think they will be able to sell the business without their employees or customers noticing and without fixing all the components of the business that may cause problems for the new owner. This is exactly why 90 percent of businesses for sale don't sell at all and why so many that do sell go for pennies on the dollar. (The good news is that, if you don't want to go through all this, Half-Retirement is actually much easier!)

About Those Off-the-Books Transactions...

A friend of mine considered buying a vending machine business. While he was examining their financials, he was told that the business took in about $60,000 in additional cash annually that they didn't report. The seller told my friend that this income came from the dollar coins his machines received. While this made a certain amount of sense, my friend was understandably leery of just taking the seller's word for it. He simply wasn't willing to pay the seller what he was asking without hard proof of all the income and then hope that the seller was telling the truth.

Bad Reasons to Sell and Good Reasons Not to Sell

There's an old saying, "Business owners don't sell for financial reasons, they sell because they are frustrated." Many owners are just fed up with working all the time or annoyed with the problems that they haven't solved yet. They don't want to sell as much as they want to unload their stress onto someone else. Unfortunately, no one wants to pay you top dollar to relieve your frustration and stress.

Other owners want to sell, because they are afraid of a downturn in the economy or another threat to their business that is completely out of their control. There is nothing wrong with weighing all options and determining that now is a good time to cash out. But selling purely out of fear will reliably lead you to bad decisions.

There are also some very good reasons NOT to sell your business, even if you're ready to stop working so much. If your kids or heirs are ready to take the reins—like I was with my grandfather's company—then handing it off instead of selling may be the right choice. But if you want to keep your asset and income while working less and enjoying life more, don't sell your business. Half-Retire!

CHAPTER 4

CREATING MAGNETISM

IMAGINE A BALL bearing rolling down a very long inclined plane. You could stop it from rolling by catching it with your finger. You could even give it a push and make it roll up the incline for a while. But sooner or later, the ball bearing will start rolling downwards again. Gravity will always win out.

Now, imagine you placed a magnet at the top of the inclined plane. Suddenly, the game has changed. Depending on how large the magnet is, the ball bearing will either slow in its descent or actually be drawn upwards. If the magnet is powerful enough, the ball bearing may race up the plane and stick to the magnet quite quickly.

The inertia of the present is like gravity working on that ball bearing. It, like gravity, will drag you down constantly, day and night, no matter what you do. You can take steps to try to fight it, but the inertia of today will always win out over Half-Retirement goals, unless you find a way to change the game.

This chapter will show you how to create a powerful magnet to overcome the gravitational pull of your business. It is about creating a force in your life that is strong enough to overpower your current set of habits and routines and draw you toward your long-term goals. In my experience with countless business owners, this is absolutely the best way to set yourself up for success.

The Science of Motivation

I can easily hear some business owners objecting to my opening metaphor by saying, "Jim, I'm not a ball bearing! I have free will! Forget this magnetism stuff. I'm just going to move forward and Half-Retire."

Trust me, I get it. As human beings, we make choices every day. Within the law and other basic constraints, we are free to make different choices if we want to. But the longer we live, the more we understand—if we're honest with ourselves—that our willpower has serious limitations when it comes to achieving our long-term goals. If this were not the case, no one would ever struggle to lose weight, read more, or save money.

Many business owners pride themselves on being decisive and strong willed: once they decide to do something, they do it. But my own experience with people attempting to Half-Retire is that it is not quite that straightforward. As long as your Half-Retirement goals are a list of things you "should" do this week, the urgency of the day will win and your chances of success are very slim.

Science offers some insight into why we struggle to do what we know we "should" do. One reason is that our willpower—according to most psychologists—is a finite resource. Our ability to force ourselves to stick to a diet or resist distractions is limited. It gets used up throughout the day, and we run through it more quickly when we're completing demanding tasks instead of easy ones.

Several studies demonstrate this. Judges make more careless decisions later in the day than they do in the morning.[19] People who use their willpower to resist eating cookies give up on a puzzle much earlier than those who haven't had to deal with that temptation.[20]

---

19   Shai Danziger, Jonathan Levav, and Liora Avnaim-Pesso, "Extraneous factors in judicial decisions," Department of Management, Ben Gurion University of the Negev, Beer Sheva 84105, Israel; and Columbia Business School, Columbia University, New York, NY 10027. Retrieved from: http://www.pnas.org/content/pnas/108/17/6889.full.pdf.

20   "Is Willpower a Limited Resource?" American Psychological Association. Retrieved from: https://www.apa.org/helpcenter/willpower-limited-resource.pdf.

Despite some recent studies to the contrary,[21] the overwhelming majority of evidence points to the idea that we're not nearly as good at sticking to our "shoulds" as we'd like to believe.

Another reason we struggle is that our brains naturally prioritize urgent matters over long-term goals.[22] When someone screams "Look out," you do not struggle to find the energy to assess the threat they are pointing out and take action, whether it's catching a falling child or moving out of the way of an oncoming car. If you don't, you will face immediate consequences in the form of a screaming kid or a trip to the hospital.

But long-term matters are much trickier. You will experience no negative consequences today if you don't make progress toward any of your Half-Retire goals. Not much will happen next month. But keep putting them off and the years can easily slip by, and your window to Half-Retire will have passed.

For many business owners, it may be helpful to think about what you would do as a leader to motivate your team toward a multi-month project. You might offer them short-term incentives, rewarding them for making progress on the incremental steps, but you would also want to make sure they had a clear understanding of the purpose of the project so they could get fully on board.

The same goes for yourself. You need to have a clear, urgent, personal picture of why you must prioritize your Half-Retirement

---

21 The well-established concept of ego-depletion has recently been called into question as part of the larger replication crisis in the social sciences. However, on balance, it still seems clear to me—and to many, many scientists—that willpower is a finite resource, at least for most people. See: "'Strongest evidence yet' for ego depletion – the idea that self control is a limited resource," *British Psychological Society* (December 14, 2017). Retrieved from: https://www.bps.org.uk/news-and-policy/%E2%80%9Cstrongest-evidence-yet%E2%80%9D-ego-depletion-%E2%80%93-idea-self-control-limited-resource.

22 Melissa Chu, "Why Your Brain Prioritizes Instant Gratification Over Long-Term Goals, According to Science," *Inc.* (July 10, 2017). Retrieved from: https://www.inc.com/melissa-chu/why-your-brain-prioritizes-instant-gratification-o.html.

every single week. Otherwise, the work associated with Half-Retirement will become a list of annoying obligations, and you will avoid them. No matter how much you tell yourself that you can push through and force yourself to complete all the steps, it's so much easier to just set your magnet and let it pull you along.

Hitting the Reset Button

At the 2016 New York Toy Fair, toy manufacturer Hasbro announced the return of a classic 1970s doll known as Stretch Armstrong. Stretch was a gel-filled action figure that looked something like a bodybuilder. As his name suggests, his body could be lengthened from its original fifteen inches to well over four feet.

Countless children spent many a rainy afternoon trying to see if Stretch could reach across a doorway or from one room to the next. Someone would pull an arm in one direction while another kid pulled a leg in the opposite. Sometimes four of us might each grab a limb and see if Stretch could expand like a parachute. And of course, the best part was that, as soon as we all let go, Stretch would return to his original size and shape. Most of the time, anyway.

Lots of business owners are just like Stretch Armstrong, pulled in every direction by their employees, their customers, and all the other demands of their business. On some days, they're able to recover significantly when they get home. But every day we pull on ourselves and Stretch, this "stretched state" becomes the norm.

This kind of life takes its toll over time. Business owners are so used to being stretched and stretched that they don't realize how contorted they are. Stretch Armstrong resets to his normal state when you let go, but your business never seems to let go. There's always something stretching you. In order to successfully Half-Retire, we need to hit the reset button and snap back into our original shape. But that will never happen until we get away from all the forces that are pulling us in a million different directions.

That's why one of the first things I suggest people do when they begin the Half-Retirement process is take some time away from the business. Maybe they have to start by just leaving earlier on a Friday. Then they can progress to taking a long weekend. Wherever you are in your Half-Retirement process, just a little extra time away enables you—like poor Stretch—to begin to remember what "normal life" is supposed to feel like. Tangible experiences of life away from work are some of the most powerful ways to create magnetism toward Half-Retirement.

Dare to Dream

The other key to strengthening the pull of your magnet is to person-alize and make explicit the benefits of Half-Retiring and the risks of delaying or failing to Half-Retire. This means you need to think in detail about the wonderful things you will get to do if you are successful, and about the specific risks you will take if you don't make progress toward your goals. By visualizing the life you will have when you are Half-Retired, you will create a powerful psycho-logical "pull" that will subconsciously move you towards that vision.

To this end, I encourage everyone to complete the Dare to Dream worksheet, which can be downloaded from our website. It asks four basic questions, two about your business and two about your personal life:

1. What work do you enjoy most? (Half-Retirement is about enjoying your time away from work as well as your time there. Through the Half-Retire process, we will eliminate work you do not enjoy and enable you to spend the bulk of your time doing the work you like.)

2. If your business could still run perfectly, what work would you stop doing immediately?

3. If you only had to work two and a half days a week, what would you do for fun?

4. If you keep going "as is," what will it cost you mentally, physically, and financially? Owning a business can take a toll on you physically and psychologically. As we age, it gets harder to meet these demands. It's not wise to assume that you can keep up your current pace forever.

As simple as these questions sound, going through this exercise is an extremely powerful tool for creating magnetism toward Half-Retirement. In short, the stronger your desire to enjoy all the good stuff and minimize your costs, the more progress you will make towards your goals. It's really not about willpower. It's about magnetism.

Hitting the Reset Button and Daring to Dream: Real Stories

Because this entire method of creating magnetism is based on personalizing risks and rewards, I want to share several real life stories from clients of mine who hit the reset button and dared to dream. My hope is that these stories will inspire you to do exactly what these people did, in the way that works best for you.

"Carl" is a fundraiser whose original business model required him to visit industry leaders in person, all day, almost every day. It worked well for him for decades, paying him a very comfortable income. The problem was that, at seventy years old, he didn't want to be on the road five days a week anymore. His wife, however, had grown very accustomed to the income he brought in and was quite resistant to making any lifestyle adjustments that would allow him to work less.

When he came to me, Carl knew his business was unsellable for all the reasons we've already covered. He was smack in the middle of every single business process, and nothing could function without him. So Half-Retirement was really his only plausible option.

The Dare to Dream exercise helped Carl see a way forward. When he thought through all the questions, he realized that he actually enjoyed talking to the industry leaders he met with; he just didn't want to drive hundreds of miles every single week to close the deals. He needed to find a way to stay part of the sales engine of the company, but not be the entire engine.

Once Carl took the time to think about it, he remembered that he had many hobbies he would love to spend more time on, such as fishing and spending time at his lake house. Given his age, he finally faced the reality that if he didn't slow down soon, he might find himself hospitalized or worse. That would leave his wife with no income at all.

The Half-Retirement process was an adjustment for Carl, but creating sufficient magnetism on the front end gave him the focus and energy he needed to follow through.

OOO

Sometimes, getting a taste of Half-Retirement when we hit the reset button gives us the spark we need to jump-start the process and see it through to the end. "Jenny" owns a very successful marketing firm, and although she didn't mind working, her husband was beyond ready to retire. When Jenny went through the Dare to Dream exercise, she was skeptical that she would ever find a way to cut back her hours. She just couldn't see how she could be involved with her business without letting it be all-consuming, and she knew if she stepped away for more than a few days, everything would fall apart.

As she thought through the questions, she determined that she loved working with clients on big picture issues. She really enjoyed coming up with new ideas and working on the overall plan. She just didn't love being involved in the sales pipeline from start to finish. She decided that if she could work less, she would stop being responsible for every single component of the proposals that were the lifeblood of her business. Instead, through a process I call "fractionalization" (that we'll cover in greater detail in later chapters), she became a resource for the people who created and completed the proposals.

Jenny knew immediately what she wanted to do with any newfound free time: she would travel with her husband and spend more time with her grandchildren, who were in elementary school. To hit the reset button, she took her grandchildren to her cabin for two full weeks. She had so much fun and created so many memories that she was immediately motivated to go back and work on the Half-Retirement process.

The risks of not Half-Retiring also became very real to Jenny during the Dare to Dream exercise. She was in good health, so she wasn't terribly concerned about dropping dead at her desk. But she didn't want to grow apart from her husband, who had expressed his strong desire that they travel together. She also knew that each year that went by, her grandchildren were getting older, and she risked missing those formative, special years.

Time is the one resource we never get more of. Realizing that your Enjoyment Years are precious and finite is one of the most powerful motivators for Half-Retirement.

Jenny turbocharged her Half-Retirement by sharing her goal with her husband. This positive trap ensured faster progress and help if she needed it. I strongly recommend that you share your Half-Retirement goal with the people that matter most to you.

OOO

"Mike" ran a manufacturing company, and he liked what he did for the most part. He wasn't ready to get out of the game just yet, but he was definitely ready to cut back. While completing the Dare to Dream exercise, he concluded that he loved the creative problem-solving side of the business. He also really liked going to trade shows, interacting with other business owners, and getting new ideas for the future.

On the other hand, Mike hated feeling like he had to drive the important business processes himself and was tired of spending most of his time at work addressing complaints. Without his presence, his employees would do their jobs, but no one would take any initiative to deal with the inevitable minor issues that popped up during the course of a work day. The problems would just fester until he returned.

Mike had no trouble figuring out what to do with his extra time. He was an avid outdoorsman and loved to bike and ski. He became very excited about filling any extra days away from work with those activities. And while Mike's physical health was fine, he knew that every day he didn't Half-Retire, he was getting emotionally worn down and had less patience and energy for the people in his life who needed him most. Specifically, both of Mike's sons were at a place in life where they really needed time, attention, and energy from their father. Mike needed to be there for them at this vital crossroads, and Half-Retirement enabled him to do just that.

OOO

"Rex" ran a technology company, and he honestly still loved to work. He got a great deal of pleasure from charting the course of the company as the visionary, and he enjoyed helping his customers leverage technology to make their lives better. He hated being the sole driver of the technological innovations needed and being the only one in the company who could reliably close a sale.

To hit the reset button, Rex took his wife on a month-long trip to Italy. This was not only an incredible experience, but it also gave him a tangible picture of what life could be like for him when he got through the Half-Retirement system. For Rex, the real risk of delay was that his wife was beginning to slow down. If he didn't progress through his Half-Retirement goals promptly, she might not physically be able to share all the experiences they were finally going to have together.

Every day when he was tempted to push his Half-Retirement to the side, Rex reminded himself that he didn't want to travel alone. That thought pulled him away from the noise of his business toward his long-term goals.

○○○

"James" ran a staffing company and he absolutely loved national parks. His bucket list included visiting every single park with his kids, who were now in their twenties. Of course, his kids were getting busy with their own lives, so the clock was ticking. When James would spend an hour on Monday mornings to work on Half-Retirement, he would imagine himself driving around a national park with his children, enjoying the majestic sights and sounds. This powerful image gave him the motivation he needed to follow through.

Why Should YOU Half-Retire?

Everyone is different. Maybe you don't want to go to Italy like Rex or drive through endless wilderness like James. But there's *something* you do want to do. Keeping that something in the front of your mind is an important part of creating magnetism.

Another component of creating the force that will pull you toward your goals is keeping a clear understanding of the alternatives to Half-Retirement. You aren't choosing Half-Retirement over winning the lottery, because winning the lottery isn't just going to happen. You are choosing Half-Retirement, because it is a more desirable option than all your realistic alternatives.

Let's break down those alternatives again, and make them personal this time:

Financial

We've already talked about how lots of owners come home from a frustrating day and are just ready to sell and be done with all of it. The problem is that, until you actually run the numbers on your business, you are comparing your very real daily frustrations with an alternative "sale" that is both vague and imaginary.

Making the financial rationale for Half-Retirement, both specific and explicit, can really help you stay motivated to follow through with the entire process. When you remind yourself of the very real value you will lose by NOT Half-Retiring, you will understand that all your Half-Retirement activities are actually earning you money in the long run.

A quick way to do this is to think about what I call the 44% Rule. In the final chapter, we mention the Acid Test, a quick, easy way to approximate the price your business could reasonably sell for, barring complications. Similarly, the 44% Rule is a fast, realistic way to estimate the return on investment you would need to obtain on the sale price of your business to avoid taking a serious pay cut in retirement.

Here's how it works. Assuming you received a lump sum payment (which, as we've already discussed, is a best case scenario) for three times your annual earnings, you would still have significant costs associated with the sale. These include fees for brokers, lawyers, advisors, and other professionals, and of course your tax bill. These expenses typically add up to at least 25 percent of the sales price.

Let's use a business that makes $300,000 annually as an example. The math works like this:

1. Annual business income of $300,000 multiplied by three yields a $900,000 sales price.

2. A $900,000 sales price less the 25 percent in expenses and taxes yields $675,000 in investible cash.

3. If you were receiving $300,000 annually from the business, you would need to make a 44.4 percent investment return on your sales proceeds, every year, just to replace the income you used to receive from the business.

Now, of course, if you have an investment that will reliably yield 44 percent, then go for it. Also, I may have a bridge in Brooklyn to sell you.

If this exercise isn't enough for you, take the time to visit your financial planner if you haven't already and ask how much money you need to retire tomorrow. The value gap between what owners need to get out of their business to retire comfortably and the price they can actually get is very real. Half-Retirement is a real and reliable way to bridge it.

Personal and Psychological

Running your business has its drawbacks, but it's not all bad. You may be genuinely tired of doing everything you're doing, but are you really ready to do nothing at all? Do you want to be a retiree playing golf and shuffleboard all day, or would you really not mind working so much if you could just get rid of all the headaches?

For many people, the thought of being a Half-Retired CEO is actually a lot more attractive than being a full retiree. Why not keep the company car, the free travel and meals, all those event tickets and other perks, while doing more of what you enjoy?

Once you take some time away to hit the reset button, you will likely discover that not only are you ready to get away more often, but you are also kind of glad that you have something to come back to. Everyone feels differently, of course, but most business owners find that they get bored without any work at all.

Also, take some time to think about your spouse, partner, or significant other. Maybe you guys really do have the kind of relationship where you want to spend twenty-four hours a day together. But for most couples, a little bit of absence can make the heart grow fonder. Don't ask me how many times I have heard a business owner say, "My spouse says 'I love you, just not *that* much.'" Remind yourself that you are working toward the goal of doing only the parts of the business you enjoy, while still making the money you've always made.

Employees and Customers

If you are the kind of business owner who develops meaningful personal connections to your employees and customers, keep those folks in mind when you are going through the Half-Retire system. Remember, Half-Retirement is a way for everyone to win, including the people who have given you and your company many great years of their lives, and the customers who rely on your work and make it possible.

Half-Retirement means you get to keep all the important people in your life happy for many more years, without sacrificing your own well-being in the process. Personalize these ideas. Remind yourself that, when you take time off to work on your Half-Retire goals, you are doing it for all the specific individuals that you care about.

Conclusion

No one but you knows what you really want out of the rest of your life. Taking time to think in detail about what you want your life to be (and not to be!) can be a powerful tool to pull you away from the demands of your business and toward the Half-Retirement that will ultimately make the life you want possible. Just as marathoners think about that slice of pizza or the warm shower awaiting them after they finish the race, leverage all these personal reasons to fuel the work of Half-Retirement.

CHAPTER 5

ADOPT A HALF-RETIRE MINDSET

WHEN THE LEGENDARY Michael Jordan came out of retirement in 2001 to play for the Washington Wizards, he was no longer the greatest player in the game. He was a thirty-eight-year-old shooting guard, struggling to keep up with the younger guys. It was Jordan's age—not his unparalleled talent, work ethic, and mental toughness—that betrayed him, just as it will eventually betray us all.

Jordan's body was ready for him to transition to a different role in the basketball world, from star player to (eventually) the owner and chairman of the Charlotte Hornets. But many of the qualities and skills that made Jordan an exceptional basketball player hindered his transition to becoming a team owner. To move on to the next phase of his life, Jordan had to let go of the mindset of a player and adopt the mindset of an executive.

Business owners need to undergo a similar type of mindset transformation in order to successfully Half-Retire. There was absolutely nothing wrong with Michael Jordan as a player, and before a torn meniscus cut his last year short, he was still averaging twenty-five points a game. But he needed to radically transform his relationship to basketball to move on to the next phase of his life. And that transformation started with the way he thought about himself and his role in the game he loved so much.

Are You Driving with the Parking Brake On?

Take a brand new [insert favorite car] out for a spin with the parking brake on, and you'll eventually start smelling smoke. There's nothing wrong with the car; you just need to release the brake so it can perform at its best. Fail to do this, and you're heading for trouble.

If your mindset is not aligned with your Half-Retire goals, it will slow down your progress like a parking brake. Align your mindset to the ones proven to work, and you will speed your Half-Retirement. I will cover common business owner mindsets that speed the launch and growth of a business, but slow Half-Retirement. Then I will cover the mindsets that will improve your Half-Retirement and show you how to remap unhelpful mindsets to helpful ones. None of the mindsets we detail in this section are "bad." In fact, many of them got you where you are today. But when it comes to Half-Retirement, it's time to release them so that you and your business can perform at your absolute best.

Here are some of the most common mindsets that can help launch a business, but undermine Half-Retirement:

"Only I can do it..."

You started your business to meet a need. Maybe no one else was meeting that need in your market, or maybe you just figured out how to do it better or more efficiently than everyone else. As your company grew, you probably still got everything done faster or better than anyone else you hired. At the end of the day, the only way to ensure something was done right was to do it yourself.

If you're going to Half-Retire, you have to put that mindset behind you. Like Jordan, you have to let go of being the leading scorer or rebounder in every game, and get ready to play a new role. Here are a few signs you have an "only I can do it" mindset:

1. **You believe you are more competent and capable than your employees.**

    - Deep inside, you feel like you're the best at almost everything that needs to be done. And you probably are. However, if you want to Half-Retire, you can't be the center of everything. The crux of the problem for many business owners is what I call "All or nothing delegation." Every business owner has special talents, knowledge, and skills that no employee can duplicate. It's work that can't be delegated.

    - However, business owners attach other work, processes, and decision-making to this undelegable work and end up with a full plate of "only I can do it." It's not a workload problem; it's a mindset problem. Half-Retire can help shift your mindset to unbundle the ordinary work from the extraordinary, undelegable work, and set you free. (Lots more on this later!) As long as you're focused on the idea that no one else is able to do things as quickly or as perfectly as you can, you will struggle to Half-Retire.

2. **You feel like the company is your baby.**

    - Babies are helpless and need a parent's eyes on them twenty-four hours a day. If you aren't babysitting them vigilantly, they could die. There was a point when your business needed your vigilant eyes on it as well. That period needs to end. When you treat the company like your baby, you feel like no one will care for it as much as you do. This is totally understandable. After all, every business runs better when the owners are in the building with their watchful eyes. You are the one who put in the late nights to nurture it from the start. It was your ideas, and your blood, sweat, and tears that brought the entire operation into being. But just like real babies are supposed to grow up, the time comes when you have to let your business go. In fact, real babies don't really benefit from having overprotective parents, and neither do real companies. We can show you how to effectively manage the business through culture, systems, and key performance indicators (KPIs) rather than vigilantly babysitting for the rest of your life.

3. **You give only yourself permission to fail.**

   - We don't classify all mistakes the same way. We think of some as understandable miscalculations or oversights, while we deem others unforgivable. It's human nature to put our own mistakes into the first category while everyone else's fall into the second, creating a culture where you are the only person with permission to fail in your company. This will cause you to have a really hard time Half-Retiring.

   - When the business was young, this mindset was helpful. After all, you were the one taking all the risk, and you had the most knowledge and talent, so your mistakes were less frequent and costly. Back then, you did not have the luxury of any financial misstep. Today, your business is not in jeopardy of folding due to a single slip-up and your people have more talent, knowledge, and insight than in the old days. It's time to loosen the reins.

- Sure, it's frustrating to watch one of your people
  make an imperfect decision that costs you money.
  However, look at the flip side. If you do not
  give them the chance to make any decisions or
  mistakes, you inhibit their ability to grow into
  the people you need, the people who won't need
  you to sit vigilantly at your desk waiting for them
  to bring you the next decision. You can't enjoy
  your Half-Retirement junket to Fiji if your team is
  pinging you with every little decision, right?

- Granted, your decision-making may still be better
  than your team's, and your mistakes less costly,
  but the cost of perfect decision-making is your
  ability to enjoy your Half-Retirement. Instead,
  give the team some "rope" and grant them permission to fail, learn, and grow.

4. **You wish everyone in the company could "think like you."**

- I find that many business owners bemoan the
  fact that their employees can't seem to "think like
  an owner." They see their own attitude about the
  company and its future as unique and the only
  one that will lead to the right decisions. Again,
  when you're just getting things off the ground,
  you have to recognize that no one else has
  invested in the success of your company the way
  you have. But as you get ready to transition into
  a new role, you must stop thinking that others
  cannot make good decisions just because they
  don't think exactly the way you do or have an
  ownership mentality.

- There's a big difference between a bad decision and a different decision. I implore you to switch from a subjective definition of a good decision to a more objective one. For instance, I might prefer to take the highway to a destination even if there's traffic, while you'd prefer the city streets. If we both get to the destination safely, does it really matter how we got there? Both ways work.

- I'm a business owner just like you, so I get it. I like my people to do things the way I see best, too. But there's a cost to getting it done exactly like I'd like. I implore you to change your standard from getting it done how you want it done to getting it done right. This will drive you nuts for a while, but if you push through, it will greatly enhance your Half-Retirement. And, please remember this:

"You can get things done the way you want them done....or you can Half-Retire."

A Culture of Urgency

President Dwight Eisenhower famously said, "What is important is seldom urgent, and what is urgent is seldom important." Urgent tasks require immediate attention, while important tasks relate to our long-term goals. Life will inevitably throw us some urgent matters now and then, but when they start to fill up entire days and weeks, we will find our bigger picture goals neglected.

If work occasionally feels like this cartoon, you may have a culture of urgency.

It's easy to drift into a culture of urgency. I've been guilty of this myself in my auto repair business. Cars came in, and they needed to be finished quickly. Many other businesses are urgent by nature as well. However, we don't have to let the business turn into a daily firefight that will rage out of control if you don't grab a hose. There are many levers you can adjust to avoid a steady stream of emergencies, from adjusting the business model, managing people differently, or simply changing your mindsets.

Here are a few signs that you have developed a culture of urgency that needs to be adjusted:

1. **You find yourself putting out fires most of the day.**

   ▪ If you are constantly racing around from one emergency to the next, you probably have a culture problem at work. It can be difficult to distinguish an unavoidable fire from a self-inflicted one, but many fires cause owner stress due to decision-making bottlenecks. You are perceived to make better decisions than your team, so processes stall at your desk and the stress piles up, just like in the cartoon.

   ▪ So how do you know if the current fire is one that requires you to extinguish it or not? When you are used to babysitting the business and making all the key decisions, every fire feels like life or death. Until you can break free from the life-or-death mindset, you are trapped at your desk and cannot enjoy Half-Retirement.

   ▪ Without getting into detail, most fires stem from a business model designed to extinguish fires instead of prevent them: employees skirting responsibility for decisions, bosses that don't allow subordinates the right to fail (and yes, this includes you as a boss), and inadequate systems.

   ▪ Every time you "jump in" and solve problems, you encourage employees and customers to put you at the epicenter of the company and the firefighting. This kind of behavior ensures you will have a constant supply of fires to be extinguished.

   ▪ Of course, businesses may go through seasons where life is chaotic for many reasons. Maybe a key employee leaves suddenly or the industry goes through an unexpected shift. These are temporary fires, not permanent ones. But if the last several years have been characterized by attending to an endless pile of urgent tasks, then that's a sign that you need to take the time to reexamine the culture of your company as a whole.

2. **You (unintentionally) value hard work over productivity.**

  ▪ Hard work is essential to getting a business off the ground, and a strong work ethic—the willingness and ability to work intensely for sustained periods of time—is a key trait of successful entrepreneurs. However, hard work is ultimately supposed to be a means to an end, not an end in itself, especially as we get older. It's easy to get there. You start with a goal and then need to put in all the hard work. This "show up and work hard all day" becomes a habit, and it seems pointless to strategize since your day is always hectic.

  ▪ Some business owners have an almost religious belief that hard work—in and of itself—will always move them closer to their goals. Sorting five thousand playing cards into red and black piles or breaking up random boulders with a sledge hammer will certainly keep you busy all day, but those activities are not necessarily accomplishing anything useful. Adjusting a single step in a business process, on the other hand, could increase the economic output of a company astronomically, even if it only takes a few minutes to accomplish. Learning to discern the difference between being busy and being productive is absolutely vital to Half-Retirement.

3. **You're a bit of an adrenaline junkie.**

- Some owners know they need to slow down, but they actually have trouble coping with a day that isn't full of action. Being slammed from sunrise until midnight might be exhausting, but it also makes them feel important, needed, and like they have accomplished something by the end of the day. They aren't quite sure what to do with themselves when they don't have a million things on their plate.

- In order to Half-Retire, you will need to separate the need to be busy from the needs of the business. It's not easy, because it feels good to know you are needed. Half-Retirement just redefines that need; it doesn't remove it. You are needed to do the things that no one else in the company can do, and when that work is done, you leave. There's no need to fill your time with work "below your pay grade" just because it feels good to be busy.

Perfectionism

Some business owners are perfectionists. This may seem like it is always a good thing, because higher quality work is always better, right? Maybe it was your perfectionism that helped set you apart from the competition, especially at first. And while we want a certain degree of perfectionism in our neurosurgeons and our engineers, in most businesses, obsession with getting everything just right will make it impossible to Half-Retire. (As I like to tell my clients, you can have everything exactly the way you want it, or you can Half-Retire!)

There are different types of perfectionism: helpful perfectionism and unhelpful perfectionism. If you are operating on my knee, perfectionism is good. If you are splitting hairs, perfectionism is probably overkill.

Most of the time, business owners enforce perfectionism on themselves and the business, not on their employees. We know that others try hard and do good work, but we can't seem to accept that same standard for ourselves.

In order to Half-Retire, you will need to distinguish when perfectionism is necessary and when "good enough is good enough" will do.

As the graph below demonstrates, the cost of perfectionism can be significantly more than the cost of good enough. You need to seize the opportunity to lower the bar a bit when good enough *is* good enough, and maintain a high standard, despite its high cost, when appropriate.

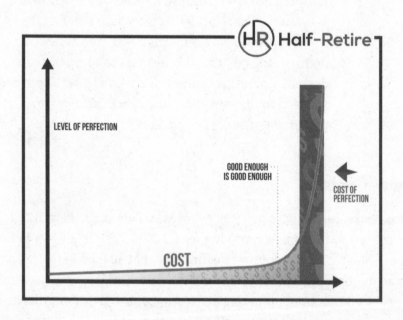

Perfectionism can also cover for a psychological need to control everything and for a fear of the unknown. There will always be a million little mistakes you can point to that prove why you can't be out of the office for long. Left unaddressed, this mindset will ultimately delay or even prevent your Half-Retirement.

Excessive Frugality

Many business owners have to watch every dollar when their company is getting started. Profits are small (or nonexistent!) and the survival of the entire enterprise depends on the owner's willingness to save money in any way possible. It's easy for the life-or-death need for frugality to morph into a mentality of "saving your way to success." I've never seen the cover of *Fortune* magazine have the CEO of the year with the caption, "The secret to my success: I took no risks, made no strategic investments, and refused to spend money even if it made good sense."

One of the worst ways excessive frugality can mutate from a helpful startup mentality to an impediment to productivity is when owners find themselves doing many tasks that are well below their skill level, simply so they don't have to pay someone else to do them. After all, it *feels* free to do it yourself.

This mindset, that can be essential for many companies at the beginning, becomes a real problem as the company grows, because it works against optimizing the use of the owner's time. To Half-Retire successfully, you will have to be willing to "buy your time back" strategically. It's an investment no different from purchasing a machine or truck. Buying your time back is an asset that you deploy to enjoy your Half-Retirement.

Owner-centric Business Model or Structure

As we've discussed earlier, many businesses evolve with the owner's skills, expertise, decision-making, and even image or identity at the center of the business model and processes. This not only risks making the business difficult to sell, but it also makes it very difficult to Half-Retire.

We will cover the process of disentangling the owner from the business model and processes in greater detail in the next two chapters. But before they even get started, owners at the center of their companies need to envision what the company would look like without them at the center. Until they do, trying to Half-Retire will be like trying to hit a target with a blindfold on.

Trusting People Over Process

"Oh, Jan handles all that. She's amazing."

I can't count how many times I hear this kind of explanation when I ask about a procedure or business system that deals with anything from payroll issues to customer service or product fulfillment. And most of the time, Jan really is amazing. But a business system built upon Jan's amazingness isn't really a system, it's a shortcut to one. As Michael Gerber said in his seminal work *The E-Myth*, the systems should run the business, and the people should run the systems. A system built upon trust in amazing people is not a viable strategy for a business whose owner is ready to Half-Retire.

The problem is that, as amazing as Jan is, she is a human being. She will not be around forever. She may decide to go back to school, stay home with her children, or move to Singapore. When she leaves, so do your systems. And then all those important things she's in charge of will be in jeopardy.

The answer, of course, as we'll cover in a minute, is that everything Jan handles should be done by a system that Jan runs, rather than depending on Jan's physical presence or unique capabilities. This doesn't mean that trust is a bad thing. But trust built on strong systems is far better than trust built on individuals alone.

And as we'll discuss in later chapters, good systems aren't something that you have to impose artificially from the outside. They actually emerge as you prepare for Half-Retirement.

Resistance to Change

It is totally natural to get set in your ways as you age, especially when those ways have brought you success. Research has confirmed that our openness to new experiences and ideas declines steadily from our twenties onward.[23] So don't feel so bad that you don't want to change the way you do invoices or follow up with leads. No one else does either.

But in order to Half-Retire, you are going to have to change the mindset that the way you've always done things is necessarily the best path to Half-Retirement. This is especially true concerning your attitude toward new technology, which can save you both time and money. Don't worry, you won't have to become a techie if that's not who you are. But you *are* going to have to learn a few new tricks to make Half-Retirement a reality.

Old Mindsets in Action

"Karen" owned a home services company and seemed to be blessed with boundless energy. She came in early, left late, and was busy every moment in between. She had a sense of urgency about everything that came across her desk, whether it was following up with new leads, finishing a job ahead of schedule, or resolving a customer service issue.

Karen wanted to Half-Retire, but she just couldn't see how to get started. None of her employees seemed to share that sense of urgency, which really annoyed her. And during the course of the day, most of them would bring something to her desk that she needed to attend to immediately. For whatever reason, they could never seem to figure out how to handle things on their own, even though they'd watched her do it a million times. This slowed down customer responsiveness

---

23 Nikolas Westerhoff, "Set in Our Ways: Why Change Is So Hard," *Scientific American* (December 2008). Retrieved from: https://www.scientificamerican.com/article/set-in-our-ways/.

and created a process bottleneck that frustrated Karen. She wanted to start taking more time away to enjoy her family and hobbies, but she was convinced that employees would make poor decisions or all the work would come to a grinding halt in her absence.

"Bill" worked about fifty hours a week for most of his life, and he was finally ready to cut back and Half-Retire. But as the only true salesman for his company, he couldn't imagine how he could possibly work fewer hours. He had some assistants who would accompany him to trade shows, but Bill was struggling to figure out how to get them more involved. To make matters worse, he still used an Excel spreadsheet for his leads, and he kept track of all his sales appointments on a paper calendar. Sure, he'd heard of marketing automation, customer relationship managementtools (CRM) , and all that stuff, but he insisted that technology wasn't his thing, so he avoided all of it. That meant many crucial business processes were literally in his hands, and his hands alone. Once Bill realized that he did not need to become a technical guru, but merely leverage technological tools as part of an improved business process, he was able to shed a significant number of work hours and responsibility.

"Mike" was beyond ready to Half-Retire. He had put it off for way too long, so once he grasped the basic concept, he was off to the races. Mike had the advantage of running a larger company that made comfortable profits, so he had plenty of resources at his disposal.

Unfortunately, Mike slipped into the trap of thinking that Half-Retirement was as simple as delegation. He took an inventory of the work he was doing, assigned those responsibilities to various employees, and took off on a long vacation.

As you might imagine, it quickly became obvious that Mike had skipped several steps in the Half-Retire process. He had technically gotten rid of his work, but he had only pushed tasks to others. That's only about 10 percent of the Half-Retire process. To offload the work *and* have the business function properly, additional steps are needed. After just a couple of months, Mike was forced to demote himself back to his old job, and he began to clean up the mess.

Half-Retire Mindsets

Karen, Bill, and Mike all discovered that they were able to Half-Retire much more quickly when they let go of their old mindsets and embraced new ones. Here are a few of the shifts and remapping that everyone must undertake to make Half-Retirement a reality:

From "Only I can do it" or "I'm not doing it, you do it" to "How should the company do it?"

When you taught your kids to ride a bike, you considered the task successful when they were able to pedal and balance without you. If your kid picked it up in ten minutes, great! If you were still holding the handlebars after a week or two, you wouldn't think your teaching had been a success, even if you were working really hard at it.

Instead of defining success as putting in a hard day's work, start to evaluate your success based on how much time you are able to spend away from your business and how long and how far your employees can pedal without you holding the handlebars. Instead of thinking of yourself as the key cog in your business, see yourself as a teacher, a trainer, and ultimately a consultant who evaluates every aspect of how things get done. Like Michael Jordan, you're not done with basketball, but you are almost done with playing on the court yourself.

From a Culture of Urgency to a Culture of Reliability

A culture of urgency is stressful for you and your team. So why do so many companies have this culture? Usually, it's so they can be highly responsive to customer needs. Ask yourself, do customers want you killing yourself with stress and constant fire drills, or do they want predictibility and reliability? The answer is the latter. Give customers what they want, when they want it, and they won't care if it did not take a fire drill to do it.

As we'll cover in the chapters that follow, once you begin to perfect your systems, you will find that your pile of urgent tasks gets much smaller. This takes time and deliberate planning, but you *can* change even the most chaotic company to an environment where emergencies are few and far between.

I have to admit, there's a part of me that likes fire drills. It feeds my adrenaline rush and makes me feel needed. That feels good to everyone, right? However, that adrenaline rush comes with a price. By shifting to a culture of reliability, you can give customers what they want and remove your hands from the fire hose. Owners whose companies have a culture of reliability are egoless; owners don't need to be at the center of activity all the time, and they know that the need to be needed works against Half-Retirement. Embracing your new role—which is no longer in the middle of all the action—is key to Half-Retiring.

From Perfectionism to Pragmatism

While the perfectionist is always looking to make things better and better, the pragmatist knows that sometimes "good enough" is good enough. Instead of obsessing over minute details that will not make much of a difference in the overall outcome of a process, pragmatic owners know how to keep things in perspective.

Of course, there are some areas of your business where good enough is NOT good enough, such as taking care of your best customer or spelling everything correctly in an expensive marketing campaign. But pragmatic owners understand that the world will not end with one or two little mistakes in an internal company email, and that employees learn best when they have a chance to do things on their own.

The concept of minimum viable product uses pragmatism vs. perfectionism. By creating a workable but imperfect product to launch, countless effort is saved until market feedback dictates the next actions. You can use the same principles on some aspects of your business to deliver what is needed, but no excess. You can then use that time saved for Half-Retirement.

This mindset shift can be a difficult one for many business owners. To them, it feels like lowering their standards to a "slacker level." Of course, it's important to be true to yourself, and you do not want to set up a dynamic of "fighting the current." Adopting a *healthy* amount of pragmatism is vital to speeding your Half-Retirement, but only you can determine the impact of a less-than-perfect solution on employees, customers, and your psyche.

You will find that the shift to a more pragmatic mindset is more of a fluid process than a flip of a switch. My experience with business owners is that they fight my pragmatism recommendation hard at first, but eventually find small opportunities to try out a less rigorous standard here and there. They then see an example like the world not ending from delivering an order in two days instead of one. Over time, the success of one pragmatic standard opens their mind to additional adjustments, and by the end of the Half-Retire process, they are much more pragmatic than they ever thought they could be.

The bottom line is that it's natural to fight pragmatism, but don't completely dismiss it. Experiment with low impact areas, and dial up your tolerance for pragmatism as you see success.

From Excessive Frugality to a Willingness to Buy Back Your Time

I recently took a cruise with my wife. At some point, the old CPA in me took over, and I calculated that each hour of awake vacation time was costing me about a hundred dollars. This is true for almost any business owner's Half-Retire time also. Why would I be willing to spend that much money for vacation when I'm reluctant to spend twenty-five dollars an hour to get help at work to buy the same amount of time or freedom?

I will speak for myself. I tend to default to cheapness. I think about saving money first and spending money second...or never. I realized that this mentality was hindering many business owners' and my own Half-Retirement. You need to be willing to buy back some time to maximize your Half-Retirement.

There's a saying I'd like you to consider as you move towards Half-Retirement.

"Just because you can do it doesn't mean you should."

You wouldn't hire Picasso to paint your house. Sure, he'd probably do an amazing job, but his hourly rate would be astronomically higher than that of even the most excellent painter who specializes in building exteriors. You are the Picasso of your business. When you do any work, you are hiring Picasso. Even if money were no object, you would not want to deprive the world of another original Picasso masterpiece, just so the master himself could spend twenty hours doing something hundreds of thousands of other people could do almost as well.

Every day you are doing work that you shouldn't be doing, you are delaying your Half-Retirement. Once you realize this, you will begin to value your time by paying others to do the work that you *shouldn't* be doing, freeing you up to do your own Picasso Work©. ***(More on this important point later!)***

From an Owner-Centric Business to Scalability

One of the most important steps in adopting a Half-Retire mindset is to stop asking the question, "How can I solve this problem?" and start asking the question, "How can this problem be solved without me or avoided altogether?" In order to untangle yourself from the day-to-day operations of the business, you have to stop thinking of yourself as the center of the business, which is how things are done today, and start thinking about how to make what you do scalable and reproducible. We will cover this process in great detail in the next two chapters.

From People-Centric to System-Centric

You've probably been relying on the talents of certain individuals to make certain parts of your business work. You want to move away from this talent-based model toward having systems in place that will work no matter who is in charge. In practice, this means you go from saying (to yourself or others), "Jan handles that issue, and she's great," to "We have a great system for that, and Jan does a great job running it."

From Technology-Resistance to Technology-Lover

Once you let go of the way you've always done things, endless possibilities open up. This doesn't mean you're suddenly writing code for the systems that run your business, but it does mean that you take advantage of all the other advances that can save you time and money. As they say, "You don't need to know how to build the watch; you just need to know what time it is." All you need is to (a) know what you want to get done, (b) have an understanding of what's possible technologically, and (c) know where to find people that can do it.

Embrace Gradual Graduation

I'm constantly asked, "Jim, how long does it take to Half-Retire?" I apologize for giving you the "it depends" answer, but it depends. For a typical business, the process can take six to twelve months. The combination of your current business situation, the strength of your magnet, your willingness to adjust your mindsets, and how quickly you progress through the program will all play a part in how long it will take. Our system can walk you through, step by step, at whatever pace you desire. Many business owners are looking for additional support and a partner to work with during this process. Should you decide you don't want to tackle this alone, I've developed a talented team of Half-Retire Coaches available to help.

That said, let's not focus on the end zone, let's focus on getting first downs. You didn't graduate from high school or college in one day. You gradually accrued credits, and the graduation ceremony was a celebration of what you accomplished in that period of time. The same goes for Half-Retirement. This is not a one-time decision or an overnight transformation. It's a process that will take time and deliberate effort. But when you are done, the results will be just as gratifying as a graduation. Remember, every credit you earned in college reduced the total number needed to graduate and gave you momentum, knowledge, and motivation to complete the mission. Every mindset you change, business model you tweak, process you adjust, and employee you train will build momentum towards Half-Retirement.

New Mindsets in Action

Karen finally faced the fact that she had unintentionally developed a culture of urgency and expected her employees to think the same way she did. As a result, nearly every business process eventually ended up in her lap by default. Unless she could find a way to get out of emergency mode, she was never going to be able to Half-Retire.

So, Karen took each task that came across her desk and asked herself: Why am I doing this? In some cases, it was because she alone had the ability and experience to handle it. In others, it was because the matter was so important that a mistake would be very costly. Then she began to ask herself a second crucial question: What do I have to do to ensure I don't have to deal with this again?

Karen had always been the "doer" in her company, but she finally began to think of herself as a teacher instead. She realized that she had not been born knowing how to do all the things she did, and her employees' inability to do anything without her help was a sign that they lacked a process and training. She had to be incredibly patient, because it took a lot longer to teach than to just do everything herself. But she recognized that the time she spent teaching was gradually graduating her towards Half-Retirement.

After some gentle nagging, Bill finally opened up to the idea that he might benefit from learning to use some new technology. I reminded him that he couldn't be all that afraid of technology since he used his iPhone pretty well and was always telling me about the latest Netflix series he and his wife were enjoying on their smart TV. Although, he did not think that my joke about him asking Alexa, "Why don't I like technology?" was funny.

Through processes we'll detail in the next two chapters, Bill was able to automate the significant data entry from his trade show visits, as well as automate a large portion of the follow-up.

This had two major effects. First, it freed up his employees to help him with other tasks. And second, it took the weight of worrying about follow-up off his shoulders. The software not only did the work, it was the system. With less to worry about and his newfound time, Bill began to spot inefficiencies in his business processes that could be solved by software. He began poking around the internet and found many further improvements. He made enormous progress toward his Half-Retirement goals, all because he changed his mindset about his relationship to technology.

Instead of easing into Half-Retirement, Mike began his Half-Retirement with a three week sailing trip. Not surprisingly, he was frustrated when he had to go back and clean up the messes his employees had made during his absence. This cemented the need for gradual graduation. Finding the silver lining, he realized that the messes had brought the weaknesses in his business to the surface, so he knew which were the most important to tackle first. I reminded Mike that problems are simply "fix me" signs. Mike learned to focus on making steady progress, instead of getting impatient with the time it took to reach his goals.

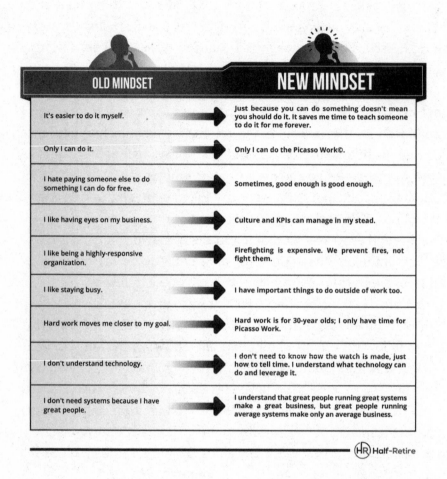

OLD MINDSET	NEW MINDSET
It's easier to do it myself.	Just because you can do something doesn't mean you should do it. It saves me time to teach someone to do it for me forever.
Only I can do it.	Only I can do the Picasso Work©.
I hate paying someone else to do something I can do for free.	Sometimes, good enough is good enough.
I like having eyes on my business.	Culture and KPIs can manage in my stead.
I like being a highly-responsive organization.	Firefighting is expensive. We prevent fires, not fight them.
I like staying busy.	I have important things to do outside of work too.
Hard work moves me closer to my goal.	Hard work is for 30-year olds; I only have time for Picasso Work.
I don't understand technology.	I don't need to know how the watch is made, just how to tell time. I understand what technology can do and leverage it.
I don't need systems because I have great people.	I understand that great people running great systems make a great business, but great people running average systems make only an average business.

(HR) Half-Retire

Change Your Mind[set]!

Changing your mindset requires deliberate effort. Just because you determine that you need to think in a different way does not mean you will automatically begin doing it. In fact, mental habits can be just as hard to break as physical habits. Our brains love short-cuts, and thinking the way we've always thought feels natural and requires a lot less energy than thinking differently.

There are several strategies you can deploy to help you change your mindset. I suggest using all of them:

1. **Work on one or two changes at a time.**

   - Most people will warn you that it is very hard to quit smoking, lose weight, read more, and get rid of all the junk in the basement in the same month. If we focus on changing one habit at a time, we'll have a lot more success. Go through the Mindset Exercise (included in the "Resources" section at the end) and determine which of the problematic mindsets you struggle with the most. Choose one or two to work on at a time. I suggest moving from the easiest to the most challenging, because experiencing success with the earlier steps can help you build momentum for the later ones.

2. **Write down what will happen if you don't change.**

   - This goes back to creating the magnetism we discussed in the last chapter. Change requires effort, so you must keep the price you will pay for not changing in the front of your mind.

3. **Utilize positive affirmations.**

   - This strategy is challenging for a lot of people who find it a little far-fetched. But positive affirmations ("I will do X" not "I won't do Y") really do work. Our brains are wired to believe what we are told,[24]

---

24   Annie Duke, "Why Your Brain Clings to False Beliefs (Even When it Knows Better)," *Fast Company* (February 11, 2018). Retrieved from: https://www.fastcompany.com/40528587/ why-your-brain-clings-to-false-beliefs-even-when-it-knows-better.

including what we tell ourselves. So, create a list of things to tell yourself ("I love technology"; "The more time I can take off, the more successful I am"), and before you know it, you'll start believing them. (For specific affirmations that will help you adopt Half-Retire mindsets, visit the resources section at the end of this book.)

4. **Don't go it alone.**

   ▪ Get help for your mindset change from employees or supportive friends. For instance, offer employees twenty dollars any time they catch you being a perfectionistic or doing work below your pay grade. If you need more help, one of our Half-Retire Mindset Coaches can help. Learn more at www.halfretire.com/mindset-coaching

5. **Be patient.**

   ▪ It generally takes at least twenty-one days to form a new habit, and mental habits are no exception. Remember that working on your mindsets a little bit every day can be very powerful over the long haul.

Conclusion

Helpful mindsets—like the strong magnetism we covered in the last chapter—are absolutely essential to the Half-Retirement process. The more you cling to the idea that only you can do certain things, that everything must be perfect, or that you shouldn't pay someone else to do something that you can do for "free," the more difficult

Half-Retirement will be. On the other hand, the more you embrace pragmatism, scalability, and your role as a teacher and a coach, the more progress you will make.

But how is all this actually going to work? How are you going to go about gradually reducing your hours until you are working only about two or three days a week? The answer lies in two key concepts: automation and what I call "fractionalization." Both of these processes will enable you to gradually untangle yourself from the day-to-day processes of running your business. And we will cover them in great detail in the chapters that follow.

CHAPTER 6

LET'S PLAY JENGA!

IF YOU'VE EVER played Jenga, you know that the game begins with a solid tower constructed of fifty-four identical wood blocks. Players take turns removing blocks from the tower and placing them on top, creating a progressively taller but less stable structure. The person whose block finally causes the tower to topple loses the game.

Jenga tests fine motor coordination and dexterity, but it also challenges each player's ability to determine how difficult a piece will be to remove and how much its removal will destabilize the overall structure. Each round presents a new strategic challenge, as players try to adjust and rebalance the tower.

The assessing, planning, adjusting, and rebalancing skills used in Jenga are the same ones you will need to take the next steps in your Half-Retirement. The only difference is that, in Jenga, all the pieces are the same size and shape. In Half-Retirement, there is one piece that is more important than all the other pieces put together: the Jenga piece called you.

The Jenga Piece Called You

Unlike the game of Jenga, Half-Retirement only needs one piece removed, the piece with your name on it. But, just like in the game, if your piece is firmly stuck and you try to force it out, your

Half-Retirement will topple. How difficult is it going to be to remove the Jenga piece called you from the tower that is your company? In Jenga, before you can remove a particular piece, you need to ensure that the weight of the rest of the tower can be redistributed effectively to other pieces. In Half-Retirement, those other pieces can be rearranged so that you can begin to ease yourself out.

To discover which pieces can be rearranged, we begin with a basic assessment of all the roles you currently play in your business. We examine every single process and ask what would happen if we completely removed you right now. How much of a problem would your absence create? What would the specific impact be? Will your Jenga tower topple?

Let's take the area of lead generation as an example. If you stopped working today, what percentage of your new leads would be lost? Depending on your role, the answer could be anywhere from 0 to 100 percent. Now, what would the impact of that loss be? Again, this depends. If you have great customer retention and no aggressive growth goals, the impact might be very minimal, even if your departure would cause new leads to drop significantly. But if you are in a transactional industry that depends on constantly generating new leads, your absence of lead production could be much more disruptive.

As we go through the list of processes, we determine which areas of the business need you the most and which need you the least. We will use the simple analogy of an easy-to-remove Jenga piece or a stuck one to denote the challenge of removing you from that particular process. Don't worry if any particular piece seems immovable. By adjusting a variety of variables, any stuck Jenga piece can be loosened.

You may feel that it's impossible to remove your Jenga piece, because you feel like you are needed everywhere. And, really, you are. But the reality is that you are vital to some processes and just helpful to others. Determining those just helpful areas is a crucial strategic decision.

Getting Started

As you begin to unwind yourself from critical business processes, remember, you do things the way you do them for a reason. At some point, you decided this was the best way to tackle the issues. You had the best knowledge available and created a good process for that point in time. In order to make meaningful change, minor adjustments or noodling around with things here and there won't cut it. You need to rethink how you do your work and how your business gets things done. This may not result in radical change; but it might. You need to be prepared to redesign any subset of your business process in order to remove your Jenga piece.

There are two ways to get started. First, download the template for a personal time log at www.halfretire.com/jenga. For one to two weeks, keep track of the broad categories of work you do. I know you think you know how you spend your days, but you are guessing. Every time a client does a time log, they get a few surprises. They were spending far less time on X than they thought and far more time on Y than they thought. Until you know exactly where your time is spent, you cannot tackle the problem.

With this data, you need to create a strategy to radically reduce your time spent on activities that eat up your calendar.

Second, you should keep a running list of everything that goes wrong when you are away. Most business owners get upset when little things go wrong. To Half-Retire, you will need to change your mindset to appreciate these annoyances, as they are "fix me signs." A process that doesn't work without you is an impediment to Half-Retirement. When the demons raise their heads out of the bushes, deal with them permanently by fixing the systemic issues.

As you change your work rhythm to discover, then systematically correct, you will create a virtuous cycle that frees up more and more of your time and loosens your Jenga piece.

Once you have done a complete assessment of your involvement in your business, you have to decide where to begin removing yourself first. I almost always recommend that clients tackle the low-impact areas at the beginning. This seems a little counterintuitive to some owners. After all, the low-need areas have the least impact on the company and you. Why not dive in and tackle the hard stuff right away? After all, it's human nature to be eager to get rid of our biggest headaches as soon as we possibly can. There are several reasons why I believe tackling the lower-impact areas first is the right choice for almost everyone. First, because they are easier, you will build momentum with early successes. Even gaining a few extra minutes a week creates a virtuous cycle where you can then invest more time in your Half-Retire activities. This will then gain even more time for you, building success upon success. Second, as you'll soon see, tackling the complex areas first can generate many unintended negative consequences.

It's all right to simply ignore problems that are anomalies. If this problem is rare or infrequent, don't give it any effort. Just cross it off the list and forget about it. There's no point putting effort into problems that may never come up again.

Every company is different, but areas that you can usually get rid of first include any low-skilled tasks that you do because they don't need to be done very often (and you become the catch-all for miscellaneous tasks) or because you are the back-up person for that job... and forty-two others. These could include anything from making deliveries, problem collections, running various errands to the bank or the post office, or "prickly" tasks no one else seems to do. Maybe you do these things during the busy season or you jump in when someone is sick. It's not easy to offload task variety, but you need to try. As insignificant as it might seem, try to redesign the work process to get rid of a portion of these tasks.

Other low-need areas include processes that run better when you are physically present at work, even if you don't do anything specific to contribute. I call this the babysitting factor, and we'll cover it in more detail in just a minute. Examples of processes that can generally run well without the owner may include areas like lead generation, finance and accounting, sales (unless you are the super-closer or you don't have a sales staff), customer service, and anything where you have a well-established, efficient system in place.

Generally speaking, the process to remove yourself from these areas is pretty straightforward. Pick one or two of these tasks and resolve not to contribute anything for a month. Then track what happens. What is the impact of your absence? Maybe it's zero, and you're not actually needed at all. Great! Move on to the next area. But if your absence did have an effect, what was it? And most of all, *why* are you needed in this area? The answers to those questions are key to getting you Half-Retired.

Once you've asked these questions, you can begin to take concrete steps to reduce the company's need for you. Some steps you can take to accomplish this are making more and better information available to your employees, providing them with better and more thorough training, and in some cases, giving up more control and decision-making power.

Sometimes it's simply a matter of letting go of your perfectionism—as we discussed in the last chapter—and with it the idea that certain things need to be done exactly the way you want them. Remind yourself that this isn't brain surgery, so a little variation won't kill anyone.

Do your best to embrace gradual graduation. A string of reliable three-yard gains may not be very satisfying at first, but they are better for you in the long run than a bunch of Hail Mary passes that fail 95 percent of the time.

Aaron versus Tom: A Tale of Two Strategies

"Aaron" and "Tom" each owned construction-related businesses, and both were ready to Half-Retire. Both men had identified the process of creating quotes for clients as something that took up a lot of their time and energy. Quote creation was a long, complicated ordeal that involved a lot of measuring, getting detailed prices from many vendors, and understanding which components could substitute for others under which conditions. Both Aaron and Tom were eager to stop doing quotes, but they took very different approaches to removing themselves from that process.

Tom was determined to get the task of quote creation off his plate all at once, so he hired Sally for the express purpose of taking over this job. Sally was a quick study, so he trained her for a day or two and then sent her off to do the work. After all, she was bright and learned quickly.

In contrast, Aaron broke the quote creation process down into every minute task and sub-task while looking at how he could reduce the time he spent on it little by little. First, he analyzed his win-percentage for all the quotes he created. He realized that there was a particular category of job that his company almost never won and that those jobs were not very profitable, even on the rare occasion the company did win them. So, as the first step in his Half-Retirement, Aaron simply stopped creating custom quotes for that category. He concluded that there was no reason to invest the time into quoting a job with a small profit margin if they were going to lose the bid 95 percent of the time. Aaron did create a generic quote packet for these types of bids rather than write them off completely. Occasionally, a prospect would want additional information and then he could make the choice to invest more time. By eliminating marginally beneficial work, Aaron was able to trim meaningful hours from his calendar.

This move immediately saved Aaron enough time to spark a virtuous cycle that enabled him to invest that time into tackling the next batch of tasks to offload. This then saved him more time that he was able to both enjoy and invest into further systematizing and training.

As you might have guessed, Tom didn't fare quite as well. Sally started creating the quotes just like she was hired to do, but, of course, she did not do it the way Tom liked and made mistakes. Tom became frustrated and fell into the non-virtuous cycle of saying to himself, "See, it doesn't do any good to get help, because it never works."

It wasn't Sally's fault. Tom took several shortcuts. There was no way a few hours of training could equip her with Tom's entire knowledge base and intuition, which he had accumulated over decades in the business. How was she supposed to know when to use which vendor and which parts could substitute for which? In most high-need areas of your business, there is an art as well as a science to getting things done. The science can be taught systematically; the art is a lot trickier.

Here's a simple trick—catch yourself using the word "should." Tom said things like, "It's not that complicated; she should know that." Or "I trained her how to do this; she should know." Whenever you are using the word "should" in relation to an employee, it's usually your fault. Challenge yourself to adopt a new mindset of taking all the blame, even if it's mostly the other's fault. Here's why—it's much easier to control your actions than someone else's.

Once you dive into the "shoulds" and attack the variables you can control, you will almost always find something you could do differently that would lessen the likelihood of failure. Rinse and repeat this process enough times, and you will solve the problem. The willingness to go through this exercise is one of the biggest differences between the most successful Half-Retirees and the rest.

Of course, Tom ended up having to circle back and approach the process like Aaron did from the beginning, but his initial decision to try to tackle a high-need area all at once cost him several months. Tom started with bold, decisive action: making a new hire and training her. Aaron started by running some numbers through a spreadsheet and then doing away with a particular kind of work. Yet Aaron made the most progress the fastest.

Never underestimate how powerful a small, simple change can be!

Addressing the Babysitting Factor

As I've already mentioned, a lot of the lower-need areas in your business boil down to the babysitting factor: processes that simply run better when you are physically present at work. The first step to freeing yourself from your babysitting duties is to ask yourself *why* the business runs better when you're around. There are usually several different reasons:

Your Knowledge Base

Just like Tom and Aaron, you've accumulated an incredible storehouse of knowledge in your years of running your business. Much of that information isn't anything you even have to think about anymore. You may not even remember how you learned it; you just know. This is why your employees find it so much easier to come to you when they have a question, rather than try to find the information for themselves. You've become the company encyclopedia, and your constant availability means that your employees aren't in the habit of figuring things out on their own. Tip: Create a company wiki or searchable knowledge base. Zoho offers a free version good enough for most businesses: https://www.zoho.com/wiki/.

The Standard Bearer

Nearly every business owner will admit to their business running better if they are simply present. You can sit at your desk and play solitaire, and it runs better, but why? Almost always, the business owner holds a higher standard than the employees. When the owner is present, the standard is higher; when the owner is absent, the standard decreases. Many business owners recognize that things work better when they are physically present and then make the incorrect assumption that there is no alternative methodology to accomplish the same results. There is a way. A full synopsis is outside the scope of this book, but you can create "culture in your stead" to secure many of the same benefits of babysitting. We will address this topic in Chapter 9: Setting the Autopilot.

Your Decision-Making and Authority

In many businesses, the decision-making process flows through the owner. This makes sense. You have the best information, the most experience, and it's your money at stake.

When you are not in the building, one of two things tend to happen: bad decisions or no decisions. Many owners complain about their teams' work-stopping indecisiveness or inadequate decision-making skills. It seems like the owners have to be on call to move things forward or too much goes wrong.

However, you can't Half-Retire if you don't fix this issue. Yes, it can be very challenging, because many decisions are so complicated. Like Tom and Aaron, you are able to make these complicated decisions relatively quickly because of your vast stores of knowledge and experience. You will need to break down your decision-making process and institutionalize it. This is a new skill for many business owners, but once you get the hang of it, you will be pleasantly surprised by all the good decisions your team can make when given the right tools and methods to do so.

Your Work

Last, and usually least, your business performs better when you are there because of the actual work that you do. Your skill, talent, and efforts move things forward, and that helps. You will keep the most important aspects of this work in Half-Retirement. The rest will take time and consistent effort to move off your plate, but that's okay. Like Aaron, a few small steps at the beginning will build lots of momentum.

To effectively address the babysitting issue, you will replace everything except the work you actually do. This means that you will no longer have to be there to be the company encyclopedia, to keep a watchful eye on everything, and to make most of the decisions. You can accomplish this through a combination of the following steps:

Embedding Your Knowledge Base in the Organization

1. Determine what information you alone possess.

    ▪ The first step in sharing your knowledge base is determining what information is so specialized that only you have it, and what information you have easily at your disposal, but is actually discoverable by other means. Sometimes your employees really need your insight, but other times they just find it easier to come to you rather than look for the information themselves.

    ▪ Tip: Adopt the 10X Rule. I used to struggle when it took employees much longer to do something than me. It seemed wasteful to have them spend an hour on something that I could do in ten minutes. Sharing information readily available at your fingertips is a great example of this. It takes you just a second to share information that it might take quite a while for employees to find on their own.

- However, as you begin to Half-Retire, this business system won't work. It's a productivity-robbing interruption that requires you to sit at your desk and play encyclopedia on demand. What worked for me was changing my mindset towards "waste." Instead of viewing an employee wasting my resources by going slower than me, I set a new bar at a 10:1 ratio. Anything that an employee could do no more than ten times slower than me was all right. Frankly, it took me years to integrate this way of being into my management style, but it's served me well ever since.

2. Write your knowledge down.

- Once you've determined which information really exists exclusively in your head, you need to write it down. When I was running my manufacturing company, I became an expert at recognizing different brake calipers out of necessity. Employees would come to me all the time, asking which part was which. To cut down on the time I spent giving them answers, I created a searchable database and photo book of the most common calipers we dealt with, along with their identifications. This enabled my employees to answer their own questions 80 to 90 percent of the time. This same process can be followed by creating training manuals for almost anything.

3. Create video resources.

    - In addition to written manuals, you can create video resources for frequently asked questions, onboarding and training new employees, and even welcoming new customers. You do not have to have expensive equipment to do this: a simple backdrop and light with a smartphone can work just fine. You also do not have to be "good on camera." Just talk to the machine the way you would talk to a person.

    - Video resources are part of what I like to call the "lawyer's trick." If you've ever dealt with a high-priced lawyer, you probably noticed that the first meeting was with the high-priced senior partner. After that, everyone else in the office took care of most of your case, while you only spent a few short minutes with the senior attorney. This is because that lawyer's time is the most valuable, so all the systems in the practice are designed to minimize the amount of time he or she needs to spend with each client to get the job done.

Reducing the Need for your Watchful Eye

1. Be pragmatic.

    - Remember that you are working to let go of perfectionism and embrace pragmatism where it's appropriate. You don't need to hang around all day just so that every single detail is handled the way you want. If they can get it "good enough" without you there, let them. Remember our saying, "You can get things done the exact way you'd like or you can Half-Retire."

2. Adjust and fine-tune your systems.

- Remember the culture of urgency we discussed in the last chapter? A lot of that can be fixed with better systems. For example, when I ran my auto-repair stores, the arrival of a new car always created an "urgent" situation, because we wanted to get the job done for the customer as quickly as possible, and I could always get it done faster. Sometimes, a job would require a massive search for hard-to-find parts. If we didn't get them ordered in before a certain time, the part would arrive a full day later, and we would be forced to keep the car overnight: a big no-no.

- This created many "fires" for me to put out during the course of a typical week, until, finally, we just changed the system. First, we made a business decision to use "scare away pricing" on certain types of vehicles that were always problematic. Second, we gave ourselves a break and changed the standard of what "get the job done fast" meant. We always went full speed, but never set a hard deadline. By allowing ourselves X amount of time for certain jobs, we could have less chaos. Third, we did a better job communicating our standard times to customers, so they could not impose their urgency on us. Sure, some people objected to the new methods, but the upside greatly exceeded the costs.

3. Standardize your processes.

    - To the degree that it is possible and reasonable, document the precise steps to follow for all of your business processes. This doesn't ensure perfect compliance, of course, but it does let everyone know exactly what is expected.

4. Cultivate a workplace culture of excellence.

    - A positive work culture is a very powerful tool for encouraging high quality, conscientious work, and discouraging shortcuts and waste. In fact, a healthy culture can actually "watch" the business for you. Any given individual is much more likely to work diligently if everyone around him is doing the same. Of course, nothing can completely substitute for your physical presence, but a culture of excellence can go a long way.

5. Identify Key Performance Indicators (KPIs).

    - Identifying and monitoring KPIs complements workplace culture as a way to watch your business when you're not there. Depending on your industry, these could include items such as the number of sales calls made, percentage of sales closed, a customer satisfaction index, on-time deliveries, or production efficiency. Think of these as the lights on the dashboard of your car. They don't tell you everything, but they do let you know when you need to fill the tank, put some air in the tires, or bring the whole thing in for maintenance.

I have a saying, "KPIs, not your eyes." As you move through the Half-Retire process, we will show you how to create a business process that relies on KPIs and other methods to eliminate the need for your eyeballs, and the rest of your body, to be at the office.

Sharing Decision-Making

1. Determine why you make better decisions.

   - Remember, problems are "Fix Me" signs. Why are your decisions better than everyone else's? It could be your knowledge of the industry, your extensive experience with a wide variety of scenarios, the fact that it's your money at stake, or your ability to think through all the possible outcomes of a decision and determine which is the most likely to occur.

   - Most of the time, it's a combination of all of these factors. Most business owners become successful after a series of trial and error decisions. Over the years, you learn what works and what doesn't, and you develop instincts others don't have. You can't

necessarily teach all of that to someone else immediately, but you can teach much of it over time.

2. Flowchart your decision-making processes.

    ▪ The next time a "Fix Me" sign pops up, flowchart
       your decision-making process. It's not as myste-
       rious or as art-like as you might think. Usually,
       your superior decisions come from a tiny bit of
       better information or an extra step in the process.
       You can teach this to your team if you get to the
       root of the issue.

    ▪ You typically make a lot of complicated decisions
       in your head, and you need to get that thought
       process out of your head and on to paper. To do
       this, you will need to create flowcharts for the
       complicated decisions you make, breaking every-
       thing down into stages. In the example of Aaron
       and Tom, the first stage of the decision about what
       price to quote for a prospective customer was
       whether or not to even bid on the job. Aaron made
       this decision by categorizing each job by certain
       criteria and calculating the win percentage his
       company had with jobs in that category.

    ▪ Obviously, if the job was one Aaron decided not to
       quote, then the decision-making process was over.
       But if he did decide to do a quote, it proceeded to
       stage two. In order to create a flowchart for the
       entire decision-making process, Aaron would
       need to show a decision tree for every subsequent
       stage, listing each of the possible outcomes.

- Fortunately, most of the decisions in your business are not as complicated as deciding what price to quote for a complicated construction job. But you still do a lot of nuanced thinking beneath the surface that needs to be clearly documented. Once you do this, you can begin teaching the process to others.

3. Identify the stronger decision-makers on your team.

- Not every team member has equally good judgment. Start paying attention to which employees demonstrate the ability to think through decisions well, along with a willingness to take responsibility for the results of their decisions. Those are the people you are going to want to begin to bring into the process.

- I also recommend not forcing decision-making responsibilities on to employees who lack the innate skill. It usually goes something like this: Sam is highly-skilled and experienced, and he's Director of Operations. However, sometimes his decision-making is a head-scratcher. You've flowcharted your preferred process, and he's still falling short. Stop forcing it. There may be a talent gap. You can teach some skills, but you can't teach logical reasoning and sound decision-making to someone who completely lacks those qualities. Find a work-around if needed, but don't keep expecting good decisions from bad decision-makers just because of their role or experience.

- Pro tip: Play the game Mastermind with your team. This game is great at teaching and diagnosing deductive reasoning. Once you learn the game, you will be able to spot those on your team with good reasoning skills and those with a deficiency.

4. Empower members of your team to make more decisions on their own.

   - Now it's time to empower the stronger members on your team to make some decisions without you. This means giving them the tools, information, knowledge, and authority to decide, as well as giving them permission to fail, especially at first. Remember to make it clear who is responsible for what, and then give them the additional information—some of which may be sensitive—so that they can make their way through the flowchart you've created for them.

   - This doesn't mean you tell everybody everything, of course. I retain certain passwords and other proprietary information for myself, even to this day. But you are ultimately going to have to share a few secrets with one or two people if you are going to spend more time away from the office. In retrospect, most Half-Retirees say that they wish they had not treated as much information as confidential, and had shared more with their team faster.

5. Determine the decision-making model you want.

   - There are two ways to approach this kind of empowerment. You can tell your team members to try to think about what you would do and then do that, or you can tell them to make their own best decisions within the guidelines you give them. I find that most business owners prefer the first option, but the plan works much better if you use the second option.

- There will be some bumps in the road during this process. If you are unhappy with a decision one of your employees has made, you must first ask yourself whether the outcome is acceptable or not. Remember the mindset of pragmatism. If it is acceptable, the best thing you can do is learn to live with it. If it is not acceptable, then you can take steps to rectify it and figure out how to fix the process so you don't get a similar outcome in the future.

Business owners with the "please think like me" method struggle with "why can't my people think more like an owner?" issue. To me, most employees will never be able to think like an owner; that's why they work for you instead of owning their own business. I encourage you to shift your thinking from "match my thinking" to "what would you do if it were your business?" If that line of thinking is reasonable, go with it. Remember, there's a difference between a bad decision and a different decision.

Tougher Areas

The areas of your business where you serve a vital function are definitely more difficult to remove yourself from. These vary from business to business but typically include any areas that rely on the following:

Your Relationships

You've spent years building up credibility and rapport with a variety of customers, vendors, and other business associates, and that goodwill can't easily be transferred to others. It takes much longer to adjust a sales system that's based entirely on your relationships than it does to tweak the way you do payroll.

Your relationships can affect many different areas, including lead generation, sales, key customer and employee retention, and vendor relations. Sometimes you are the only one who can effectively manage a valuable but difficult employee, just like you may be the only one who seems to be able to make a particular customer happy.

Your Experience

Your experience also cannot be easily transferred to someone else. When there's a major problem or a major opportunity, your years of experience running your company will give you a wealth of knowledge and intuition about how to handle it.

Your Leadership and Strategic Thinking

Your leadership gifts and ability to think strategically for your company will most likely remain part of the work you continue to do while you are Half-Retired. However, your leadership may also make you the best at recruiting, hiring, and training employees. It will take some time and planning to untangle yourself from these processes.

Other High Skill Tasks

Other high skill tasks vary greatly from industry to industry, but they include things like high-level finance, any talent deficiencies on the team you're compensating for, and any highly skilled employees you fill in for sometimes. While your business is still young, it makes sense for you to be the backup CFO, the backup salesman, or the backup proposal writer. But once you're ready to Half-Retire, you will need to become the third or fourth option for those positions, not the second.

You are actually going to use the same strategy as you did in the low-need areas to remove yourself from these high-need areas. Namely, you are going to slowly start taking time away from each process, determine where the weaknesses are, and then make the needed changes. However, because these new areas are so much more complicated, you will utilize what I call the FEVER process, which we will cover in detail in the next chapter.

As you gradually remove yourself from your company, continually check your mindset. Are you being perfectionistic or keeping yourself busy for the sake of being busy? Are you treating the business like your baby instead of letting it grow up? These are signs you may be falling back into a pre-Half-Retire mindset and causing yourself frustration or unnecessarily slowing your progress. Stay true to the Half-Retire mindsets.

And most of all, be patient with the process. Embrace gradual graduation. Focus on making incremental improvements, building momentum, and pushing through to the end. In the next chapter, we'll show you how.

CHAPTER 7

IT'S TIME TO CATCH THE FEVER!

NOW I'M GOING to show you how to do the impossible. It's time to unload that crazy, specific, undelegable work: that complex bundle of (and often annoying!) tasks that just can't be done without your special experience and expertise. And we're going to tackle it the same way you eat an elephant: one bite at a time.

We will be applying the same overall strategy to the more challenging work that we discussed in the last chapter: removing the lower-impact, easier components first, and then using the time and energy we save to make the larger changes. After coaching hundreds of business owners through the Half-Retire process, I have developed the acronym FEVER to help them remember a key tool for task removal.

FEVER STANDS FOR:

Fractionalize

Eliminate

Virtualize

Expedite

Rethink

First, we'll reexamine why the work you do cannot be delegated. Then, in the sections that follow, we'll look at each component of FEVER in greater detail.

Fact: Your Work Cannot be Delegated

Yes, you are reading this correctly. I'm saying that, in its current form, your work *cannot* be delegated. I have never met a business owner who wasn't both carrying way too many responsibilities and eager to get rid of at least some of them. So why is it so hard? Have you not considered delegating your work? Of course you have. Are all business owners just that bad at delegating? Of course not. The problem isn't the motivation or willingness to delegate. The problem is the work itself.

Your work may be undelegable for several reasons. First, what you do consists of a complex bundle of tasks that involve completely unrelated skillsets and experience. Second, your work involves some infrequent tasks that are necessary but don't come up every day or even every week. Third, your work requires a level of skill that only you possess (or that only you possessed at the time the work became part of running the company). And fourth, your work requires access to proprietary information and permission to fail, which again, only you possess.

There may be other reasons your work cannot be easily off-loaded in its current form. If it requires a trusted relationship, it's not very easy to hand off to someone else. You may also do highly consequential work with little to no room for error. Fortunately, all these problems can be addressed with fractionalization.

Fractionalization: The Trick to Making Delegation Actually Work

Getting rid of the difficult-to-offload work that you do is not a straightforward job. It is not even five straightforward jobs. Those difficult-to-delegate jobs are an incredibly complex bundle of tasks that you perform without thinking. Fractionalization—as I use the term[25]—refers to methodically unbundling these tasks, and then breaking them down into their smallest possible subtasks, determining what work is undelegable (your Picasso Work©), and systematically offloading the rest.

Finding your Picasso Work© is one of the secrets to Half-Retire. Picasso Work© requires your special talent, genius, or experience. This undelegable work is highly valued by the organization and typically takes very little of your time once you fractionalize your work. By acknowledging that you and only you can do certain work, you will forever change *how* you offload your work.

Once you have done this, you can rank each subtask according to difficulty and need for your special skills. Spoiler alert: today, it feels like *everything* requires your special skills. After all, why else would you be doing that work? However, when you attack your work from a fresh perspective, you can unbundle the generic "work" into tasks and subtasks, discovering ever smaller pieces of work that do not require any of your special talent. You can then begin to offload them. As with other components of the Half-Retire process, you will get rid of the easiest pieces of work first and use that extra time to develop training for the more difficult work.

---

25   I realize that "fractionalization" has entirely different meanings in social science, linguistics, and physics. For the purposes of this book and all my courses, it carries only the definition laid out in this chapter.

For example, consider the very easy task of changing a lightbulb in a particular light fixture. The subtasks involved might include:

1. Selecting the correct lightbulb from its storage location

2. Carrying the stepladder from its storage location to the light fixture

3. Walking safely up the stepladder

4. Removing the old lightbulb

5. Inserting the new lightbulb

6. Walking safely down the stepladder

7. Disposing of the old lightbulb appropriately

8. Replacing the stepladder in the storage location

Breaking the process down into so many steps might seem like overkill. Who doesn't know how to change a lightbulb? It seems like second nature to you and a one-step process—change the bulb—but imagine you were the only person who knew where the lightbulbs and ladder were stored, plus the only one with any money to purchase new bulbs. Most people bundle all of these steps together, because they *can*. They have the special knowledge, skill, and permission for all of it. Typically, an employee doesn't. When you unbundle the work that really does require you from the work that doesn't, you can transform undelegable work into mostly delegable work. In addition, the work that is stuck on your desk isn't lightbulb changing. It's a complex bundle of diverse tasks that you have bundled into "lightbulb changing" over the years. It's this task bundling that makes work feel undelegable when portions of the work can be offloaded.

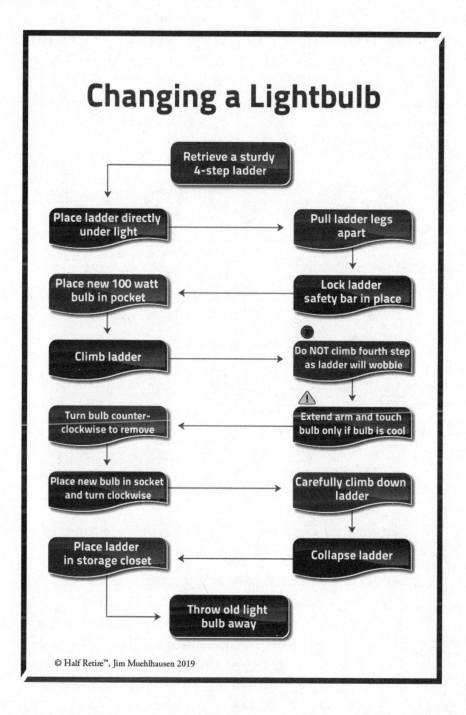

Changing a Lightbulb

Retrieve a sturdy 4-step ladder

Place ladder directly under light

Pull ladder legs apart

Place new 100 watt bulb in pocket

Lock ladder safety bar in place

Climb ladder

Do NOT climb fourth step as ladder will wobble

Turn bulb counter-clockwise to remove

Extend arm and touch bulb only if bulb is cool

Place new bulb in socket and turn clockwise

Carefully climb down ladder

Place ladder in storage closet

Collapse ladder

Throw old light bulb away

© Half Retire™, Jim Muehlhausen 2019

Think about each specialized task you complete with the level of detail you would use to teach it to new employees. This will take a little longer on the front end, but it will greatly reduce the mistakes you have to deal with in the future. When in doubt, err on the side of being more specific. Remember, what seems like second nature to you is new and complex to others.

Pro tip: I find that people who have ever programmed a computer are much better at breaking down tasks than most business owners. Here's why it's harder to describe how to do something to a robot or computer vs. a human being. We say things like, "Well, they already know that," or use "shoulds" when describing a process to another person. A robot knows nothing, so the level of detail and precision has to be better. My advice is to use a flowchart and create a process for a robot.

Why Traditional Delegation Doesn't Work, Especially for Entrepreneurs

Traditional delegation is 100 percent/0 percent: someone else does 100 percent of the job, and you do 0 percent. This all-or-nothing delegation method usually fails, because no one can do the work that requires your special talent. I call this work your Picasso Work©. Fractional delegation is 98 percent/2 percent: someone else does 98 percent of the work, and you keep that 2 percent which is Picasso Work©. By not attempting to delegate the entire task, the process is set up for success.

I cannot overemphasize the power of 98 percent/2 percent delegation vs. all-or-nothing delegation. Many business owners have given up on delegating much of the work they do, because they have been burned so many times before. It usually goes something like the diagram below, ending with, "Never mind, I will just do this bundle of tasks myself."

The reason that offloading has failed before is because you tried to offload the entire bundle (100 percent), including your Picasso Work©. No one else will *ever* be able to do your Picasso Work©. By giving up trying to delegate your undelegable tasks, but insisting upon delegating the rest, you can break free of your unwanted work.

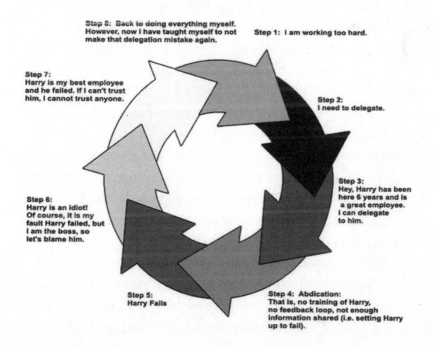

It's completely natural to dream of getting rid of your difficult or annoying tasks all at once. That's how traditional delegation supposedly works, and it is immensely appealing. But remember Tom in the last chapter? He tried to offload the entire process of quoting prices for prospective clients all at once. Not only did it not work, it also set him back in his Half-Retirement process by several months.

The reason it's so hard for entrepreneurs to delegate their work is that all-or-nothing delegation ignores the Picasso Work©. A painting cannot be sold for millions of dollars unless Picasso touches his brush to the canvas. The rest of the process does not require Picasso's work, but without that one critical piece, the business model breaks down. You have your Picasso Work© too. It's undelegable work bundled into many other tasks.

By giving up on the prospect of delegating *all* of a task, you break free of the challenges of all-or-nothing delegation. By retaining your Picasso Work©, but delegating the remainder, previously undelegable tasks become delegable.

Think about it this way: how would you have fared in math if your teacher had tried to teach you arithmetic, algebra, geometry, and trigonometry all in a single month? Even if you were a math genius, you undoubtedly would have struggled to learn this bundle of skills all at one time. It took your math teacher many years to learn all that material, and it would be unreasonable to expect you to pick it up in a matter of days or weeks.

But that's exactly what you're doing when you try to offload complicated and bundled tasks all at once. You are giving your employees jobs that took you—in all likelihood—several years to develop, and asking them to learn them over a period of days or weeks. That's a recipe for frustration and failure.

Instead of learning math all at once, you mastered the basics and then moved on to the next level. You learned arithmetic with whole numbers and then progressed to fractions and decimals. Later you tackled algebra. Most likely, your teacher didn't let you move on until you'd **demonstrated mastery** of what you'd already been taught. That is exactly how fractional delegation works.

Instead of dreaming about being free of all your work immediately, focus on what you can offload today. Once you've gotten rid of some of those easier tasks that we discussed in the last chapter, you should have enough time and energy to devote to fractionalizing your remaining work.

Four Quadrants of Work

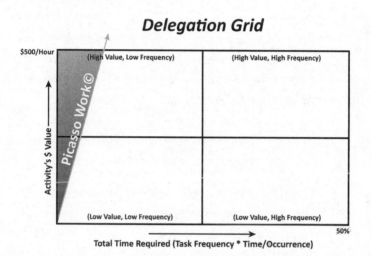

Delegation Grid

Many business owners find it helpful to classify business tasks into four quadrants, as shown in the above illustration. You often do the low frequency, low skill work, because it's really not worth delegating while you're still coming into the office every day. Some of these tasks only take a few minutes each month, but they do need to get done.

High frequency, low skill work is anything that can be taught to almost any employee in a relatively short amount of time. High value, high frequency work can also be taught, but only to talented, capable employees. And the low frequency, high skill work is what you will keep as your Picasso Work©. This is the work that you enjoy, that only you can do.

The Five Stages of Fractional Delegation

Once you've divided a job into its smallest component subtasks, there are five major stages to the fractional delegation process:

1. Offload subtasks that are easy to learn and master (20 percent)

   - As we've discussed, you will start by offloading the tasks that require less skill and time to complete. These are tasks you can teach any employee to complete successfully in less than a day. You can expect these tasks to comprise about 20 percent of your overall workload.

2. Offload subtasks that high-aptitude employees can master relatively quickly (50 percent)

   - In this phase, you will tackle the tasks that talented, competent employees can learn to complete with relative ease. This phase is absolutely essential and will entail deliberate instruction on your part. You can expect these tasks to comprise about half of your overall workload. You will also notice that you can increase the volume of work you offload in this stage by hiring better talent. (Our coaches can help you assess and improve your hiring process, if needed.)

3. Offload subtasks that must be learned by osmosis (20 percent)

   - Some processes can only be learned over an extended period of time, by observing, absorbing, and asking questions. To offload these tasks, you will select key employees to work with you over a period of weeks or even months. You can expect these tasks to comprise about 20 percent of your workload.

4.   Offload tasks that can only be mastered by very highly skilled employees (8 percent)

   ▪   Toward the end of the delegation process, you will offload tasks that can only be performed by your most talented, capable employee or employees. These typically comprise about 8 percent of the workload.

5.   Keep your Picasso Work© (2 percent)

   ▪   After you have completed the previous stages of fractional delegation, you will be left with the last 2 percent, which you will keep as your Picasso Work©. Yes, you will intentionally not delegate this work. These are the tasks that only you can do or that you enjoy and do not want to give up. You will complete them during your time in the office while you enjoy your Half-Retirement. Keeping your Picasso Work© is one of the secrets to Half-Retirement. This ultra-high skilled work adds tremendous value to the business and takes minimal time, so it won't disrupt your Half-Retirement.

Imagine you try to Half-Retire without identifying and leveraging your Picasso Work©. For example, some potential Half-Retirees try to hire a replacement CEO. Sure, you can hire a seasoned pro to sit in your chair, but he or she won't have your experience, connections, or institutional knowledge—that is, your ability to do Picasso Work©—which can doom the plan in many cases.

I'd love to tell you that this process always goes quickly and smoothly, but it will in fact take time, patience, and deliberate effort on your part. Keep the 10X rule in mind: if an employee can complete a task in ten times the time it takes you (or less), then you should go ahead and offload the task. With practice, they will improve their speed and efficiency. Remember: it's only wasteful if it doesn't save **you** time!

Fractionalization in Action

Lots of business owners spend countless hours working on proposals. Much of the work is similar from proposal to proposal, but they want to make sure that the finer points of the proposal (pricing, terms, special insights) are perfect. Those details are the difference between winning and losing the bid. The owner isn't going to be able to Half-Retire if they can't boil down this proposal process to Picasso and non-Picasso Work. In the ten-hour process of creating the proposal, only thirty minutes might be Picasso Work©. Without unbundling and fractionalizing the process, they are stuck doing all ten hours of work.

"Kevin" owned a business that required him to sort alternator cores on a regular basis. This was a highly specialized task that took him an entire work day every single week. It was a classic example of the kind of intricate, challenging work that takes years to master and is very difficult to offload.

Kevin dreamed of the day that he didn't have to look at another alternator core again. He was very tempted to just hire a couple of people and hand the job off to them. But he knew that if they misidentified a single part, that mistake could cost his business thousands of dollars. In short, sorting alternator cores was not only an incredibly high-skill task; there was virtually no room for errors of any kind.

This is why the mental "bundling" of tasks is so dangerous. Bundling makes us believe that many discrete tasks are only one task and thereby makes it impossible to delegate any portion thereof. As you learn to recognize your Picasso Work©, you will be able to fractionalize and unbundle the rest of the tasks and break free of tasks you thought to be undelegable.

For the first step of the fractionalized delegation process, Kevin got some employees to simply help him with the work. They brought him parts and put the parts he identified into different piles as he instructed them to do. This was easy work, and it saved him about an hour each week. Even though Kevin was paying two employees to work six or seven hours to help him save an hour of his own time, this fell within the 10X rule, so it was worth it. Kevin reminded himself that his long-term goal was to work half-weeks, and this was just the first step to get him there.

Next, Kevin created a picture book of all the General Motors alternator cores and began teaching a couple of employees to identify them. He started with GM parts, because he had determined that these were the easiest to recognize, and they accounted for about 15 percent of the total parts he dealt with in a given week. This meant that once his employees learned the GM parts, Kevin saved another hour of his own time.

Kevin carefully monitored the accuracy of his employees, testing them frequently. Once they had mastered the GM parts, he taught them the rest of the American manufacturers. All the American manufacturers put together made up about 50 percent of the parts he dealt with, so now he was down to spending less than four hours a week on sorting.

Next, Kevin selected one particularly gifted employee, "Kyle," and had Kyle work with him during the four hours that Kevin was sorting alternator cores each week. He didn't bother to teach him the oddball parts that came up only once every few months. But by the end of a few weeks, Kyle was capable of accurately sorting 90 percent of the alternator cores that came into the building.

It's important to note that Kevin intentionally withheld the most difficult work from Kyle. It's a common mistake for business owners to throw too much variety and complexity at employees when offloading work. This almost always ensures failure. The employee is forced to deal with too much, too fast, and can't master anything. I have a saying that may help you remember this as you are offloading your work, "It's only the work employees can do without HELP that is HELPFUL."

Kevin was down to what appeared to be the undelegable work, the identification of the oddball parts that only came through infrequently. However, Kevin got very creative and applied fractionalization to this particular microtask. His Picasso Work© was the ability to look at a chunk of metal and instantly know the part number. Everything else needed to be offloaded.

So, Kevin taught his employees to line up all the unknown parts and place them in a particular position so that he could identify them without even touching or rotating the part. Once a week, he would come out to the department with a team of employees with paint pens. Kevin would call out the part number, and the employees would write the number on the part so it could be identified permanently. The employees then whisked the parts away and placed them into inventory. A job that had once taken Kevin eight full hours now took him an average of fifteen minutes each week.

Now, what if Kevin had tried to unload the entire task of sorting alternator cores all at once? Most likely, his employees would have become overwhelmed and incorrectly performed some portions of the work. Instead of learning to recognize the parts in a logical progression—from simple to complicated—they would have tried to learn everything all at once. They would have inevitably made mistakes and cost the company tens of thousands of dollars.

Kevin started simple, focused on building mastery, and saved the outlier parts for himself as Picasso Work©. He knew it was more important to teach a smaller percentage of the parts perfectly than to teach all the parts with an unacceptable margin of error. Kevin was successful because he was a methodical, patient, and clever unbundler. Do the same, and you can succeed in fractional delegation.

Rethinking and Eliminating Tasks

You've probably heard some variation of the story about an old woman who always cut off the end of the roast before she put it in the oven. Her daughter grew up and got married and did the same thing whenever she served roast. One day, the daughter was serving *her* daughter dinner, and the little girl asked her mother, "Why do you cut the end of the roast before you put it in the oven?"

The woman thought for a moment, and answered, "I don't know. Grandma always did, so I guess that's why I do it, too."

Later that week, the woman called her mother and asked her why she cut off the end of the roast before she put it in the oven, and the grandmother replied, "Because the pan was too small to hold the roast without cutting it first."

The lesson here is that sometimes our preferred method of getting something done outlives the reason we developed the method in the first place. I like to call these "unwritten rules." We don't know why the rules exist, or even why we follow them; we just do. While working toward Half-Retirement, we need to be like the little girl who asks, "Why do we do it this way?"

During the Rethinking and Eliminating stages of the FEVER process, you will examine every process in your business and ask five questions:

1. Are we inadvertently following unwritten rules, and if so, what are they?

2. Why do we do this the way that we do?

3. If we had to do this another way, what would that be?

4. How can we restructure the process so I am involved much less?

5. Do we need to do this at all?

Often, you will find that there are components you can rethink—such as the frequency of meetings you attend—and eliminate without much cost. For example, suppose you change your weekly staff meeting to an every-other-week meeting. If you will lose only 10 percent of the benefits by doing so, while cutting the time you spend at the office in half, then you're coming out ahead. As you prepare for Half-Retirement, you will scour your business for these kinds of tradeoffs.

Work That Doesn't Add as Much Value as it Costs

Imagine you were thinking of replacing the windows in your home. You get estimates and determine that the cost will be around $20,000. How would you make the decision to replace the windows or not? You might just look at your bank account and decide if you want to spend the money. But a smarter homeowner would estimate how much the new windows would save on heating and cooling costs, and how much they would add to the resale value of the home.

If the new windows would save you a couple hundred dollars a month in utility costs and significantly boost the resale value of your house, then they are probably worth the investment. If it would take you fifty years to make your money back, then you might want to pass on that particular renovation.

You need to go through the same process of evaluation with all the work processes in your business. Are there processes that you are in the habit of completing that take a lot of time and effort without adding much value? Are there activities that might have been important at one time but have outlived their usefulness? It's time to rethink the way you do them, and whether they need to be done at all.

For example, lots of information is nice to have, but not necessarily worth the time it takes to extract. Some testing procedures, specification reports (that don't include KPIs), information obtained at trade shows, and in-person meetings with prospects may all yield helpful data, but the usefulness of that data doesn't justify the cost of your personal time once you're ready to Half-Retire.

In addition to cutting employee meetings in frequency, you may be able to cut the amount of time you are actually in the meeting. High level executives—including the President of the United

States—are often in key meetings for only a few minutes. Don't worry about appearing rude or self-important. There are plenty of ways to handle this kind of arrangement respectfully and kindly.

When time and energy are unlimited, we tend to shoot for "the best it can be" as the standard. That's an admirable goal and great for pre-Half-Retirement. Once you reach Half-Retirement, however, the "best way" may no longer be the best way, once you consider the effect on your time. Keep your pragmatic mindset, and remember that, for some things, good enough is good enough.

Keep your overall goal in mind as you rethink and eliminate: getting yourself out of the office. Is everything going to run exactly the way it used to? No. Your absence will carry a cost. There's no way around that reality. Your goal in rethinking and eliminating is to minimize that cost, not eliminate it.

Rethinking and Eliminating in Action

A professional speaker colleague of mine gave about a hundred speeches a year. As you can imagine, this resulted in a grueling travel schedule. When he was ready to Half-Retire, he completely rethought his company, giving only a handful of speeches a year when the opportunity was massive. The rest of the time he worked, he did online training, which took up far less time and involved no travel at all. By eliminating travel and rethinking how he generated revenue, my colleague was able to dramatically cut his workload without sacrificing income.

Another client was a homebuilder who carefully analyzed all his divisions as he prepared to Half-Retire. He concluded that his property management division consumed a lot of his team's time and energy, while causing the bulk of the headaches. As an added bonus, the division made very little profit, so he gave it away to a competitor. By shedding the division, he could redeploy his time and his team's time to more profitable activities without costing him much money.

Expediting: Assess Your Efficiency

In my experience, most entrepreneurs are pretty efficient. We have spent years cramming an impossible number of tasks into a finite amount of time, and somehow almost everything gets done (most of the time, anyway). Almost all of us have experience with both multitasking and time blocking, and we typically finish the day satisfied with our productivity.

But all that doesn't mean we can't improve our efficiency. The first step to using our time more effectively is to determine how we actually spend our time. We all know teenagers waste hours on social media or surfing the internet, but as adults, we also struggle to allocate our time to our top priorities. We never get on the computer with the intention of being inefficient. It just happens. Most business owners aren't spending hours playing video games, but many of us are spending way too much time answering emails or dealing with relatively routine matters.

Fortunately, there are many simple solutions available to help you improve your efficiency. You can begin by installing a monitoring app like Rescue Time on your computer, phone, and tablet. It runs securely in the background and tracks the time you spend on various applications and websites. Whenever you want to see how you are spending your time, it will generate daily, weekly, and monthly reports. You can also complete a time log for each day, to track how much time you spend on which activities.

Many kinds of project management software enable you to plan, assign tasks to yourself and others, and set due dates for those tasks. The program will then take care of sending out reminders at the intervals you choose. There are also many great books on efficiency and productivity. Two in particular that I have found helpful are *Getting Things Done* by David Allen, and *Algorithms to Live By,* by Brian Christian.

Once you've identified activities that steal or waste time, set positive traps for yourself to help you avoid them. Start by telling employees or your spouse to hold you accountable for your goals. You'll probably find them more than willing to stay on your case!

One of the most important lessons of the expediting stage is that your work expands to fill the time available. If you are in the office for eight hours, there is no way you will *not* find activities to occupy you the entire time. On the other hand, if you only make a certain number of hours available, you will often find new ways to accomplish things much more quickly.

One of my clients, "Sandy," was struggling to get certain time-intensive work done on a regular basis. She made a commitment to work on it every Monday, but no matter how hard she worked on her other tasks, she never seemed to finish early enough to get to it. The work was important but not urgent, so it always ended up at the bottom of the pile.

With our help, she began to approach the problem differently. Instead of getting to work at eight AM on Mondays and trying to complete her urgent tasks as quickly as possible, she began to do the time-intensive work at home. Then she would arrive at the office at one PM, and somehow, she was still able to get everything done before she left. Simply showing up at work five hours later than normal enabled Sandy to expedite her Monday workload. A large block of uninterrupted time, plus the intentional delaying of the daily work tasks, created a double whammy of productivity. Sandy was more productive at home with a distraction-free workplace, plus she completed her checklist-types faster, because she contracted the time to complete them.

I define a positive trap as a cause you intentionally set in motion that will make your desired goal more likely to happen. For instance, I inadvertently set a positive trap for myself when we had outgrown our house. I told my wife something like, "Hey we aren't really in the market, but let's look at a few houses." To my surprise, a month later, I owned a new house. I should have known I had set a cause in motion. I have seen many savvy business owners use positive traps to help them accomplish their goals faster and easier. I strongly suggest you add this tool to your arsenal. For instance, I created the halfretire.com website when this book was just a concept. I knew writing a book was a must-do item, so the pressure of showing the concept to business owners on the web created a positive force to get this book done sooner.

Like Sandy, you can decrease the amount of time you make available for certain tasks. You can fill the extra time with non-urgent but important work (like Half-Retirement planning!), or you can fill it with recreation. Either way, you will find yourself becoming more efficient very quickly.

Virtualizing

We've all heard about the automation revolution and robots taking everyone's jobs. Wouldn't it be great if a robot could take part of your job? For owners of non-tech companies, these coming changes can feel remote and irrelevant. There are significant ways, however, that almost any business owner can harness current technology to make tremendous progress toward Half-Retirement:

Automation

Maybe you can't automate your manufacturing or deliveries yet, but there are almost certainly some time-consuming processes that you can make more efficient (or reduce your involvement in) by utilizing automation. Processes that involve repetitive tasks are primed for automation. These may include data entry, payroll, payments to vendors, and even marketing, which we'll cover in more detail in a later section. Companies like Zapier have helped businesses automate previously manual computer tasks by integrating disparate software packages.

Maximizing Videography

For decades, science fiction movies and television shows have shown us a future where we can send digital holograms of ourselves across the galaxy to communicate and connect with people (or aliens!) millions of miles away. Although current three-dimensional projections don't look quite as good as they do in *Star Wars* or *Star Trek*, the rest of that technology is already here.

For many business owners, videography is a powerful tool that enables them to be many places at once, connecting with customers and employees while simultaneously relaxing at home or on a beach somewhere in Hawaii. Unlike a paragraph in an email, in a manual, or on a website, a video recording of you captures your personality and enables your customer, employee, or prospective hire to get a sense of you as an individual. It lets some of your special genius shine through.

A common problem for business owners is "People want to deal with me." In sales, customer service, or even dealing with employees, your face-to-face interaction is vital. So how can you Half-Retire if your face-to-face interaction is life or death to the business operation? Virtualization via videography is the answer. Sure, a video of you isn't the same as live interaction, but in many cases, it will do well enough to allow you to Half-Retire.

With a few hundred dollars of equipment, you can save countless hours well into the future. I suggest clients begin to block off time for recording videos on at least a few of the following topics:

1. FAQs

   - When I force clients to analyze the situations where they feel they need face-to-face interaction, they come to the sometimes unpleasant realization that they are saying the same things over and over again. Their work is mostly unvaried; it's the person receiving the information who changes. If this is true for you, and it probably is, start a running list of standard answers or scripts you use and record them.

   - One of the first topics I have our clients complete videos on is answers to frequently asked questions for customers and employees. Once you record an answer to a particular question, you've answered it forever. You—or an employee—can simply send out the video-recorded answer every time that question comes up. You can do the same for customer service issues and prospective FAQs.

2. Onboarding New Customers

    -   Recording a welcome video for new customers or clients is a powerful way to connect with them without spending any extra time. It's an efficient way to give a personal touch, even during your Half-Retirement. Imagine a video welcome from the owner for every new customer.

3. Recruiting Employees

    -   Prospective employees can get a good sense of you and your company and what makes you special when you utilize videography to share information with them. This gives you a leg up on the competition as you are giving more robust information to prospective employees than just words on paper.

4. Marketing Proposals

    -   Many software programs enable you to create marketing proposals—complete with images and information—with video narration from you. These can be personalized for new prospects and are often much less time consuming than trying to coordinate an in-person meeting. Our coaches can share examples of these and teach you how to create them if you need help.

5. Updates for Customers and/or Employees

- Much of the information you might have communicated in a meeting or on a call can be shared with a video. This lets you offer a personal touch from anywhere in the world. Check out loom.com to create quick and easy video voicemails that enhance your message.

Marketing Automation

The internet has changed consumer buying habits in ways that would have been unimaginable just a few years ago. Customers now like to be able to browse information and learn about products and services on their own, without the pressure and hassle of actually talking to a salesperson. This means that you can both automate and personalize a great deal of your marketing process, saving you time and money.

For many businesses, the fundamentals of the sales process have changed from a human-driven process supported by marketing to a client self-education process augmented by salespeople. This shift in buyer preferences can be a great help to your Half-Retirement. By shifting your sales and marketing process to accommodate the self-selling that customers prefer, you can move to a process that's much easier to manage.

The right kind of marketing automation takes your prospective customers through a standardized process that often includes some sort of quiz or questionnaire. Each question is adjusted based on their earlier responses. By the end, you have a much more complete picture of their needs, wants, and resources, and how to best serve them.

By enabling prospective customers to browse information about your company, enter their information, and sort themselves into the appropriate categories, you save yourself (and your employees) phone and data entry time. You are immediately protected from directly dealing with low-priority prospects, and you can assign different categories of prospects to the appropriate employees. Your system can then send follow-up communications—tailored to that particular customer's interest—at the intervals you choose. Almost all owners report that this kind of automation leads to higher quality marketing and follow-up.

Remember, you can also easily coordinate your online advertising, CRM software, revenue planning software, and data mining programs so that your marketing, sales, client relations, and revenue tracking work together almost seamlessly. These kinds of automation changes take some getting used to, but they are very doable for anyone, regardless of technical expertise.

I call this an information ATM. Today's customer does not want to be sold; they want to self-sell or self-educate. Many businesses fight this, because they believe that personal interaction works best, and it does....IF the customers will let you interact with them. It's awfully easy to hide behind a web browser and be anonymous. By creating an information ATM for prospects, customers, potential employees, and your team, you can create a better business process while saving yourself countless hours that you can deploy on the beach.

Email Solutions

Many companies take advantage of delayed email services, which enable them to craft various emails all at once and then have them sent out at the appropriate times. These could include marketing and sales follow-up, as well as communication with employees or customers.

I also advise my clients to consider having at least two email accounts, one that I call the "Bat-phone" (remember the old television show with the red phone that went straight to Batman?) for friends and family and important business contacts, and one for everyone else. Back in the days when our mail was delivered exclusively through the post office, executive leaders would always have assistants who opened their mail and sorted it for them. Multiple email accounts enable you to have an assistant respond to professional correspondence that doesn't require your individual attention, while keeping your personal emails private. This can save you valuable time and speed up your Half-Retirement.

The Stress Test

After you've made some progress offloading your more specialized work, you will want to put your changes to the test. And the test is very simple: think about how long you believe you could be away from your business without anything going wrong, and then go away for a little bit longer than that. Generally speaking, this will be between one and five days. During that time there are only two rules:

1. No checking in with the office, no phone calls, no emails. As far as everyone is concerned, you are somewhere without cell reception or internet.

2. Have fun!

Before you go, assign a trusted employee (or two) to gather information about what happens in your absence. Which systems run smoothly? Which are a disaster? What exactly goes wrong and why? When you return, have the employees report their findings to you. It's probably a good idea to give them a promise of immunity from any problems that occurred in exchange for total honesty.

No matter how much you trust your employees, however, you will need to consider the possibility that they are skewing their reports—knowingly or unknowingly—to suit their own interests or agenda. If your reporter works in accounting and has been gunning for a software upgrade for months, don't be surprised if the report shows that the upgrade is absolutely essential.

The next step is to determine the root causes of the problems. Is it the personnel? The systems? Do your employees lack certain information? Is it a deep systematic issue or one that just requires a few tweaks? Once you've decided the answers, you will focus on the causes that have obvious solutions and address those with what we call "forever fixes." These are solutions that ensure the problem never happens again.

Remember that everything that went wrong in your absence is just a "Fix Me" sign, pointing out what you need to do next. The most disturbing report you could receive is that nothing went wrong at all. This means that either your employees were not being honest with you or they were not paying attention.

Offloading your most specialized work may sound complicated and intimidating at first, but in reality, you just need to give it enough time and effort. Remember to work through every step of FEVER. Start with the easier tasks, and let your early successes build momentum to tackle the more challenging ones. Stay focused, keep repeating the process, and you will find yourself Half-Retired sooner than you think.

CHAPTER 8

RE-LEVERAGING ASSETS

YOUNGER READERS MAY not remember that Netflix began its life as a service that mailed DVDs to its subscribers every month. When internet speeds grew to the point where video streaming became affordable and available to the masses, Netflix was able to leverage its brand and customer base to become a leading provider. And as of this writing, it is leveraging its cash, stock price, and growing subscriber list to produce thousands of hours of original programming, racking up fifteen Oscar nominations in 2019 alone.

While Half-Retirement may not require you to completely reinvent your company, you are going to need to consider re-leveraging some of your key assets. Why? Because you are removing a portion of the most important asset of all: you. While you are traveling, hobbying, and enjoying yourself, your business will be missing the value of those hours you used to punch the clock. That economic value needs to be replaced, or your income could go down.

Don't worry. This isn't as dramatic or as complicated as it sounds. To replace the value that your presence and skill add in the office all day, you will follow a very simple process. First, you will discover an underleveraged asset. (Don't worry, you have plenty!) Next, you will rethink the role that asset can play in your business. Then, you will demand more from that asset, and lastly, you will systematize the new way that asset is deployed, tweaking and adjusting the processes as necessary.

Examples of Underleveraged Assets

Re-leveraging your assets is vital to the Half-Retire process, because it replaces the value lost by your reduced workload. This, in turn, allows you to put these funds to work protecting your Half-Retirement. For example, most CEOs have routine work as part of their pre-Half-Retirement routine. While the Half-Retire process can eliminate or reduce the volume of these tasks, you may need to add staff to offload this work. Most businesses are utilizing their key existing staff at full capacity, so adding more work isn't possible.

I call this "buying your time back." If you want to offload the work, someone else will need to be paid to do it. These funds don't magically appear; you have to create them by re-leveraging assets. There are countless examples of underleveraged assets, but here are some of the most common:

Hidden Gem Employee

The hidden gem employee is someone who has untapped talent or efficiency that isn't being utilized to its full potential. You may know right away who this is in your company, or you may need to create some opportunities to take on more responsibility and see who rises to the occasion. Many times, a hidden gem employee can contribute in ways you never imagined. One client had a cash crunch and had a rank and file shop worker invest his sizeable recent home sale proceeds as a minority shareholder. Two years later, this previously anonymous employee was managing the entire production process. By giving employees opportunities to "step up," you can find hidden talent within your existing staff.

Of course, sometimes the hidden gem employee is you. I had a client who was a sales trainer, and for most of his professional life, he sold his services on an hourly basis. But when he was ready to Half-Retire, he realized that his hourly wages didn't effectively leverage his exceptional skillset. He moved to a value-based pricing model that shared the profits he helped create and effectively tripled his billing rate.

This re-leveraging had two major effects: first, it dramatically increased the amount of money he collected for each hour of work. Second, it encouraged him to focus on higher quality clients, since he was now reaping the benefits of their increased productivity. By re-leveraging his own talents and time, my client was able to work less than half the time he used to, while actually increasing his income.

Underutilized Employee Time

Your top employees may be fully utilized, but there are usually some employees who are not as utilized as they could be, not because they are being lazy, but because you are not demanding as much as you could from them. I'm sure you have heard the adage, "The work expands to the time allotted." It's true, and your people are filling all their time. However, they probably can do more work or more efficient work if you take the time to examine it. This is a great area to re-leverage because your ultimate goal is to grow the capacity of your team—in both time and talent—to handle most of what you are doing right now.

Don't feel like doing a full-blown exam-
ination of the team's work? Try simply
adding more work to staffers who you
think may have additional capacity. You
will be surprised how many employees can
handle additional work simply by asking
them for more. I had a terrific assistant,
Angel, at my manufacturing company. She
started as a warehouse helper and eventually became second-in-command.

She was hardworking and always busy,
but I followed my own advice and kept
adding work to her plate. To my surprise,
she kept finding ways to get it done.
When she finally came in my office and
said, "Enough already," I had doubled or
tripled her workload. It was a win-win, I
got greater productivity, and she got the
chance to demonstrate that she was a star
worthy of more responsibility.

Re-leveraging your employees' time doesn't have to involve radical
steps. One of my clients had a company that sold replacement
windows, which involved sending salespeople door-to-door. This
was not a popular job, but he had a team of competent employees
who did it consistently and effectively. He was able to re-leverage
his sales team by allowing other companies to pay him to offer
their services as well. If prospective customers weren't interested
in replacing their windows, for example, a team member would
then offer gutter cleaning or lawncare, or whatever the new client
company did.

Occasionally, getting rid of a troublesome employee can add value to Half-Retirement. During the last recession, I noticed a lot of my clients remarking that their businesses ran much more smoothly with less time and energy from management. This was because financial constraints had forced them to get rid of the least productive employees. This led to fewer problems and better leveraging of everyone's time, including the owner's. You can harness this "recession effect" by becoming less tolerant of employees that make more problems than they solve or make your Half-Retirement more difficult.

During Half-Retirement, you don't have the luxury to deal with prima donna employees, excessive drama, or people who cause more problems than they solve. Sometimes it can make sense to cut your losses. If you have employees who meet these criteria, ideally, you should figure out how to reform them or get rid of the employee and absorb the work with the existing team. If you have to get rid of them, it could create a double win. You save the salary and you regain the time, energy, and effort once devoted to the problem employee. If you have to replace the position, bite the bullet and do it early in your Half-Retirement. If you kick the can, you will still have to do it later, and you will lose years of benefits of the problem-free employee.

There are two kinds of employees: ones that take problems off your desk and ones that put them on your desk. It will be tougher to Half-Retire if you allow employees to create problems that only you can solve.

A friend of mine, Steve Shaer, wrote a great book on this topic, *Fix Them or Fire Them*. It's a quick read and provides a great blueprint to turn a problem employee around or move on. His step-by-step process to terminate an employee is a must read if you don't have a full-time human resources professional on staff.

Firing Customers

Are you open to the possibility that proactively choosing to not do business with certain customers can actually improve profitability and reduce operational stress? This move isn't for everyone, but everyone should, at least, consider it. Half-Retirement requires optimization and high-efficiency. Occasionally, you have a customer that sucks far too many valuable resources from the organization in exchange for the margin they generate.

By looking at every facet of the customer delivery experience, sometimes you can find that firing a customer is a simple way to re-leverage your employee time or other assets. Look at everything required to service each customer and not just the sales or margin generated. Does your staff hate working with them? Is every delivery an emergency? Do they pay late or nickel-and-dime you? Do you need special processes or equipment just for them? There are dozens of factors you can examine.

After you have looked at all the financial, psychological, and human capital costs of doing business with every client, you may find that some customers are unprofitable or low profit. This is a big opportunity. Effectively, you can create the "Recession Effect" I mentioned earlier without the pain of an actual recession. Remember, transactions create costs, not sales. That is, it's not the dollar volume of the sale that is directly related to the cost of delivery; it's the work you need to do to deliver the sale. By eliminating marginally profitable transactions and their associated work, you can streamline operations, ditch problem employees, and get back to your core competencies. This can speed your Half-Retirement and make it less stressful.

Remember, sales themselves don't drive costs; the number of transactions do. By eliminating customers whose transaction costs are disproportionate to the profit they bring, you reduce stress on the organization and on yourself.

Business Model

True or false: all business models erode over time.

Unfortunately, it's true. There may be newer and better ways for your company to achieve a profit that you have yet to implement, which we'll cover in the later section on rethinking your business model. However, if you can already point to your own particular "tricks of the trade" that yield profits for your business, then you may have proprietary information that you can re-leverage to your advantage. One of my client's businesses offered tenant screening services to landlords, and had a unique algorithm for finding the type of landlords who were particularly open to their services due to demographics and timing. She was able to leverage this trick, while maintaining the trade secret, by selling advertising space on her weekly postcard mailing to other companies offering services that complemented her own.

In some cases, your current business model may make Half-Retirement difficult. I knew an accountant who switched from a traditional practice model to a pure bookkeeping model, because it was less dependent upon his time, and the offering was more productized than the previous service model.

Another client had a fleet of service trucks running all over town fixing problems on demand. This business model involved a lot of firefighting (figuratively speaking), and the owner was the best firefighter available. This made it stressful and difficult to take time off, as some fires could not be extinguished without the chief firefighter. He tried to hire a replacement "firefighter." Predictably, twenty-five years of experience couldn't be learned overnight, and it did not work to his satisfaction. After three attempts to hire his replacement, he changed his business model to shift as much business as possible to a preventative maintenance model. This wasn't as simple as it might sound, and he came up with an ingenious plan that shifted 60 percent of on-demand customers to a preventative maintenance route. This easier-to-execute business model was the magic that allowed him to enjoy a stress-free Half-Retirement.

One of my clients manufactured a remarkable fire-retardant product, with multiple applications that they had not come close to maximizing. While the owner was eager to re-leverage this product in Half-Retirement, he knew that marketing was not one of his company's core competencies. Rather than attempting to rectify a weakness, he formed a strategic partnership with a box company that was able to incorporate his flame-retardant product into their boxes. One of the first comarketed products was a laptop box which radically reduces the risk of lithium batteries potentially catching fire aboard air cargo planes. If this happens, an entire airplane can be set ablaze in a very short timeframe. The box company took care of the marketing, and both companies gained immensely in sales and profitability. By radically shifting the sales model, he sold more products and cut "selling time" from his calendar.

Intellectual Property

My client "Devin" ran a company that managed gas station change-overs, the process by which a single station changes its banner from one company to another (Shell to Exxon, for example). This happens much more often than you might think, and Devin's company manages hundreds of these changeovers at a time. To maximize efficiency, they developed a phone app that enabled them to easily monitor all the pesky details with the touch of a finger. When it came time to re-leverage his assets, Devin realized that this app did much more than manage internal operations. A slightly modified version could be used to manage all sorts of projects for major retailers. He now markets it to firms dealing with retail giants like Walmart and Home Depot, increasing his income without adding any time to his workweek.

I've also re-leveraged intellectual property in my own business. I had a training package that I had designed specifically for one of my business units, but by adding just a few extra components, I was able to make it applicable to a much wider range of clients. The sale of that training now comprises a large share of my income, as opposed to under 5 percent in its previous form.

Brand

If your company is a trusted name in your community and readily recognizable, you can potentially discover additional ways this brand power can be further utilized to your benefit. One of my clients had a powerful seventy-five-year-old brand that he wasn't really taking advantage of. He grew up with three-step distribution where he sold his product to an original equipment manufacturer (OEM), who sold it to the distributor, who sold it to the customer. He knew there were opportunities to sell directly to distributors and end users, but he was looking for less work as he prepared for Half-Retirement. Instead of seizing the opportunity internally, he rented the domain name out to another business for an annual fee and a percentage of the profits that the site generated. This was found money, as he had no intentions of offering the brand on the web.

Relationships

Your relationships with customers, employees, and other businesses or vendors are very important assets that can be re-leveraged in many different ways. You have spent many years investing in relationships important to your business. These relationships pay dividends every day in the form of devotion of employees, orders from customers, or expedited shipping from a vendor. However, these are just examples of the inadvertent leveraging of these relationships. Digging deeper and creating a plan to extract more than the incidental value can be a powerful support to your Half-Retirement.

I had a client who had a series of unfortunate events and suddenly needed $250,000 for payroll in a few days. Desperate, he asked his next-door neighbor for a loan and got it. That trust and instant financing ability of his neighbor had been there for years, but my client had never needed to ask. What leverage can you gain from your relationships by simply asking?

Finances

If you have a significant amount of profit or cash on hand, you have a great deal more flexibility to plan and execute your Half-Retirement. You can redeploy those resources in a variety of ways—like Netflix making their own movies and television shows—and you can also invest that money to buy back more of your own time.

Hard Assets

Real estate, machinery, vehicles, equipment, and other hard assets can all be redeployed for your Half-Retirement. Maybe the office space you own is now in a prime location, but location doesn't matter much for your business. A client's building had become a prime location as the town grew, and the building was a bit too small, so he sold the building and rented space in an industrial part of town for a fraction of the cost. The same goes for any vehicles or pieces of equipment that aren't constantly in use.

Even though one of my clients in manufacturing had industry-best equipment, he was no longer able to compete with Chinese labor costs. Instead of throwing in the towel, he formed a joint partnership with a Chinese manufacturing company. He shipped his equipment to the partner's Chinese location. The Chinese company got use of the best equipment in the world, and my client's company got a share of the profits instead of watching his equipment gather dust.

Another client of mine is a real estate developer in Northern Virginia, where office space has become astronomically more expensive over the past two decades. Instead of continuing to pay hundreds of thousands of dollars in rent on his office building for employees who spent most of their time in the field, he created more than enough office space by sectioning off some of his ten-thousand-square-foot home and paving a second driveway. This saved him enough money to Half-Retire without sacrificing any income.

We all do business in a dynamic environment, so all of our assets become underleveraged over time. This means we need to take stock on a regular basis to determine how they can be better deployed to serve us in Half-Retirement. We have worksheets to help you do this, available for download on our website.

In addition to the kinds of examples given above, Half-Retirement is the perfect time to rethink your people model, your business model, and your operations model to ensure that you are getting everything you can out of your business. Once you've assessed all these components of your business, you may be shocked to discover how much unrealized potential you've been sitting on over the years:

Rethinking Your People Model

Every business is different, so every business owner will need to rethink his or her people model differently. What do I mean by your people model? How you reward, manage, motivate, and interact with your people all determine your people model. With a new people model, the overall goal is the same: you want to retain good people, attract better people, and put all of them to work in a way that will serve you well in Half-Retirement. There are several guiding principles that will help you do this:

Greater Transparency

During Half-Retirement, you should consider shifting your people model to one where you share more information with your employees than you have in the past. This means you will begin sharing what I like to call "CEO data"—contacts, costs, lists, and so on—with your team. This is uncomfortable for many owners because giving up more information means trusting more and giving up a level of control. But the inescapable reality is that, if you want the team to perform as well without you as with you, they must have access to every insight you do. Anything less is asking the team to perform with one arm tied behind their back.... Giving your team better information in greater quantities will increase the volume, efficiency, and quality of their work.

Sharing more information with your team is essential to cultivating a sense of ownership of the company's goals and future. Jack Stack, CEO of SRC Holdings Corporation, shot to fame when his company's stock price soared an unbelievable 292,000 percent.

Stack "attributes [his] success to his open-book management policy which, according to SRC, calls for 'transparency, integrity, and business and financial literacy' and allows for every employee to have real stakes and accountability in the company."[26]

Stack ended up turning the most mundane tasks into games for his employees, complete with rules, goals, and bonuses. You can do the same with your company, but you will likely have to share more information with your team than you do right now. How can your sales team close deals without you if they don't have access to your contacts and relationships? How can they begin to think strategically if they don't have a deeper understanding of your expectations and goals for the company? Greater transparency is the answer.

Expanded Decision-Making Power for the Team

As we discussed in chapter 5, to Half-Retire successfully, you will need to let go of being the sole or primary decisionmaker for many of your business processes. In practical terms, this means forgiving your employees for making a mistake the way you would forgive yourself. It also means becoming more flexible and pragmatic.

When empowering your team to make more decisions, ask yourself: What is the easiest way for them to make more decisions *without my input*? Remember, the endgame here is for things to run smoothly while you're out of the office for extended periods of time. If you find that you can't trust people in key positions enough to empower them to make more decisions, it may be time to consider replacing at least some of them.

Sometimes you can actually hand over the reins to employees and assume the role of "CEO Emeritus." One of my clients owned

---

26   Rob Dube, "Winning the Game: Jack Stack on Why People is the New Critical Number," Forbes (November 27, 2018). Retrieved from: https://www.forbes.com/sites/robdube/2018/11/27/winning-the-game-jack-stack-on-why-people-is-the-new-critical-number/#b55376d3c11b. For more, see Stack's terrific book, *The Great Game of Business: The Only Sensible Way to Run a Company.*

several branches of a children's gym franchise. His adult daughter was ready and willing to step up from her current role and oversee the day-to-day operations, enabling him to Half-Retire, and take on an advisory role. Another business owner owned a dozen auto-repair stores. When he was ready to Half-Retire, he sub-franchised them to his general managers. Each manager began to function as an owner—without having to invest the initial capital usually required—in exchange for paying my client 10 percent of their sales.

Talent Growth

One of the most important ways you will re-leverage your assets in preparation for Half-Retirement is to grow your team's talent. This will require an investment of time, energy, and resources into training, mentoring, and formulating the correct incentive structures. Right now, you may be saying, "Jim, wait a minute, isn't Half-Retirement about putting in less time?" Yes, but it's also about shifting where you invest your time. By reducing your time spent on the day-to-day activities, you can reinvest that time into talent growth and the people that will help your Half-Retirement work well.

To do this effectively, you will need to get to know your team better. What are they good at? What skills do they need to improve? And perhaps most importantly, what motivates them?

The answer to this last question may seem very straightforward: people want money, and more is always better. But real-life motivation can include many other factors and varies greatly from person to person. While money is undoubtedly important to most people, some will happily trade some money for greater flexibility and freedom over their time. Many people want prestige and power at least as much as they want money. Others value challenging or meaningful work, while still others place great importance on their work environment. There are many different assessment tools that can offer you greater insight into how the individuals on your team are motivated. These can be found on our website.

To increase and sharpen your employees' skills, consider sending them to outside training courses. Although this will cost some money up front, it has several advantages. First, it requires very little time from you. Second, it gives them a chance to hear many of the things you have probably been telling them, but from a new authority with a different perspective, which will greatly increase the chance that they will follow through. Third, it shows you are willing to invest significant resources in them.

I would ask for a short, written report from the employees you send to outside training, asking what they got out of it, why it was beneficial, and what they intend to change about the way they do their jobs. This holds them accountable not only for paying attention, but also for the changes they intend to make in their behavior. We have several courses we can recommend, depending on your team's specific needs.

To make the best use of the time you spend mentoring, begin to select the employees in whom you see the most leadership potential. I often suggest owners set aside one lunch each month for a mentoring session, allowing the mentee to drive the topics you cover by asking questions. Don't overthink or over-structure these sessions. Just share how you think about things, how you go about making decisions, and other helpful insights you have picked up along the way. Simply spending quality one-on-one time with these key people will drive positive change.

You can also have your team members work with you for certain time periods, just like my client Kevin did when teaching his employees to sort alternator cores. This should not be confused with the traditional understanding of "shadowing." Shadowing is code for, "We don't have a training system so I guess following someone around is better than nothing." You can do better than that. Having employees follow you around and passively observe is almost always a waste of man hours. Instead, give them specific work to do, helping you or doing what you are doing with you directly observing. This is how a lot of focused learning takes place.

Developing your team's talent will be beneficial to everyone involved, but remember that your priority is to do it in the way that best serves your Half-Retirement. This means looking for the largest pockets of untapped potential: the people who will become significantly more productive with more training.

Some clients have been unpleasantly surprised by employees whom they believed were high-potential assets to aid in Half-Retirement. The employee had the potential to grow, earn more money, and help the owners Half-Retire, but they lacked the motivation. These clients wasted valuable time wishing the employee would "step up," only to be disappointed. Here's my two cents: Half-Retirement offers great opportunity to employees with the skill and desire to step up.

Whether they do or not is up to them. Don't delude yourself or waste time ignoring the signals that a particular employee isn't interested; move on. I promise you will be disappointed by an employee that does not step up, but pleasantly surprised by another who does and greatly exceeds your expectations.

Talent Acquisition

Most mid-sized businesses can't compete financially for top-tier talent, so many have become adept at finding employees with growth potential and turning them into stars. This is an asset!

If you have the ability to take average candidates and make them great, you need to leverage it more. If you do not know how, I'll give you the quick overview.

The first step is to distinguish between skills and traits. Skills include things like the ability to use a particular software program, and to perform certain tasks that are often industry-specific. Traits include character qualities like reliability and maturity, as well as more innate characteristics like personal charisma and the ability to learn quickly.

It's very tempting to recruit for skills, because they are what you immediately need. But where are you going to find individuals with the precise skillset you're looking for? Probably at your competition. And like you, your competition is working hard to keep their best workers, so you will (most likely) be recruiting their rejects or at least paying top dollar for them.

So, I advise my clients not to look for "plug and play" recruits. Instead, hire for traits and train them with skills you need. Think about some of your great people. Did you hire them as a plug and play employee, or did they grow into a special contributor? 90 percent of the time, owners tell me some story like, "I don't know why I hired Marcia, but I just did. She really wasn't qualified, but I saw something in her. Five years later, I don't know what we'd do without her." We are looking for more of those, and they come by hiring according to traits and aptitude.

There are many ways to assess traits and aptitude in the interview process, including cognitive assessments like the Wonderlic Test, and Predictive Index Test, or personality tests like Myers-Briggs or DiSC assessments. Some employers look for recruits who have played and enjoyed team sports, knowing that such individuals will be good team players. Others look for people with a certain level of commitment to the job, who do not mind taking calls in the evenings or working weekends.

A client has a hard time getting employees that will take weekend calls, so she conducts all interviews on Saturday morning. Many candidates disqualify themselves with their unwillingness to interview on a Saturday. In her mind, it was good riddance.

Talent Acquisition in Action

A client of mine, "Stephanie," needed to hire a person with strong sales skills. Based on the demographics of the population this person would be serving, the ideal candidate would be an attractive, assertive, experienced saleswoman. But Stephanie was recruiting in a market with full employment, and the going rate for an experienced salesperson was well into six figures, which was more than she was able to pay.

So, we helped Stephanie come up with a plan to recruit the traits she needed, and train the skills. She asked herself, "Where can I find people with these traits and offer them a better way to use them?" She went to buy perfume at one of the local department stores, and waited to see which of the young women selling perfume was most assertive.

She bought perfume from "Nicole," and then asked if she wanted to double her current salary.

I call this strategy fishing in a different pond. Stephanie was able to recruit and train Nicole to do the job she needed. Instead of getting a mediocre salesperson from the pool of employees that her competitors were recruiting from, Stephanie found a hidden gem in a different pond.

This kind of story is a good example of why you shouldn't rely on a resume to tell you everything that you need to know about an employee. Resumes tell you what a prospective employee has done, not what he or she is necessarily capable of.

For this strategy to work, however, you have to be willing to invest real time and effort into training. You can't just throw talented recruits into the deep end of the pool to see if they can figure out how to swim. Talented individuals want to feel competent and prepared to do their jobs, so you have to thoroughly equip them to make that happen. If this is one of your areas of great need, we have a supplemental course that covers how to create a hiring and training system, which is available on our website.

Culture

Another important part of rethinking your people model is determining the kind of workplace culture you want to cultivate. You will need a strong culture to reinforce the behaviors you want and to motivate people to continually work toward the long-term good of the company. What makes your company great? What makes it special, setting you apart from the competition? Zero in on these unique qualities to determine how you can best institutionalize them.

We'll talk a lot more about cultivating a culture that can babysit in your absence in the next chapter.

Rethinking Your Business Model

As we've discussed already, your business model is the system you use to make a profit. This may be distinct from what you sell, at least as far as your customers are concerned. You may be focused on how much you pay for that airline ticket, but the airlines make much more from seat and bag fees. Major League Baseball was not profitable in the early years, because they thought their business model was selling tickets to games. Once they figured out that the real money was in selling hot dogs and beer, they were able to make a profit. Your favorite restaurant may have a razor-thin margin on the steak you just ate, making all their profits on the Coke or the margarita you ordered.

You can rethink your business model in several different ways. One is to find a way to increase your profit margins without raising prices. Another is to rethink where you actually get your profits. Still another is to lower transaction costs or the number of transactions you have to complete to get the same (or close to the same) amount of income.

One of my clients, "Ralph," offered power washing and general construction services and had crew "dead time" like many service businesses. Ralph began to use his crew to renovate houses during slow periods, which he then resold or used as rental properties. This was an additional profit model that enabled him to afford to Half-Retire.

Another client ran a chain of retail stores and had a small fleet of trucks to make deliveries to his various locations. His trucks were never full, so he began renting the extra space to a well-known beer company that needed to make deliveries in the same area. When he was ready to Half-Retire, he realized that the deliveries he made for the beer company were actually more profitable than his own deliveries. So, he redesigned his truck routes to add more beer routes, and prioritize the beer deliveries, while still providing his chain of stores the items they needed.

"Ken" owned a company that serviced outdoor lighting at stadiums, parks, and other venues. One of the largest drivers of their costs was sending technicians to change lightbulbs at a single venue. This cost around $350 a visit when the technician visited one location and returned to the office.

Unfortunately, there was really no way to arrange for all the lightbulbs they serviced to burn out at the same time at venues that were located near one another. And of course, most facilities couldn't afford to wait a long time to have their lightbulbs changed due to safety concerns. If Ken couldn't keep their lights on, what did they need him for?

So, Ken rethought his business model. Instead of sending out technicians to replace lightbulbs on demand, he created a program where companies signed up to have their lightbulbs proactively changed on a regular basis. This way, Ken was able to send technicians out to change several lightbulbs at once, all in the same geographical area, while still giving his clients what they needed: a guarantee that their lights would always be on.

This small change cut Ken's average cost per visit from $350 to $220, enabling him to Half-Retire. Just one of his clients didn't like the new system, so that client and Ken parted ways.

To discover where you may have untapped potential in your business model, you can analyze each of its components. As we discussed in chapter 3, there are three major components to your business model: your offering, your monetization (profit model), and your sustainability. You will want to review each in detail during this phase of Half-Retirement preparation. On our website, you can find detailed worksheets to score your business model in each of the three areas.

I will cover business models at only a high level in this book. If you are interested in a deeper dive into the topic, feel free to check out my book *Business Models for Dummies*.

Scoring Your Offering

Your offering is exactly what it sounds like: the products and/or service you offer your customers. How highly you score your offering is related to three factors: industry attractiveness, niche attractiveness, and customer attractiveness. For instance, software firms tend to have better margins than construction companies. Those industries have more attractive factors in general. Your niche within your industry can affect attractiveness.

Verizon Wireless caters to customers who need great coverage and don't mind paying for it. Boost Wireless caters to the opposite niche—customers who want a cell phone at the cheapest price and don't care about speed or coverage. Selling to some customer segments is more profitable than other segments. Attractive customer segments will score your offering better. What are the best customer's characteristics? Do they buy regularly, pay on time, and refer you to others? Remember, you don't necessarily need wealthy customers, just faithful ones. Walmart, McDonald's, and other companies do just fine by serving customers who do not necessarily have high incomes, but do purchase regularly.

High-end doesn't necessarily equal a better business model. Walmart has a more successful business model at the low end of the market than Neiman Marcus does at the higher end.

The second main component of the offer is your unique value proposition. This is comprised of four subcomponents: product potential, marketability, the unique selling proposition, and brand power. Is there untapped potential in your product or service, or is it end of life? Is your product highly marketable or difficult to market? The more you can market a product instead of being forced to sell it, the better the score.

So how can you adjust the offer to make it more marketable? Why do customers choose you over your competitors? It might be the quality of your deliverables, your speed, your customer service, or your reliability. How can you sharpen your differentiation and deliver more of what the customer wants? Maybe you've developed a unique brand power over time, or your company is uniquely marketable for some other reason. All these qualities can be re-leveraged.

Monetization

Monetization refers to both your profit model and your sales model. Your profit model is where you actually make your money. How do you monetize your offer better than competitors? How can you improve? Gas stations make almost no money on the gasoline itself; some even choose to take a hit and sell it to the customer at a little below cost. Their profit comes from the candy, soda, and cigarettes they sell to customers buying gas. No one needs candy, but everyone needs gas. By selling what people need at a thin margin or even a loss, gas stations are able to make a profit on what people want.

This profit model extends to many other retail industries. Grocery stores offer milk and certain staples as loss leaders to get customers into the store. The all-you-can-eat buffet in Las Vegas is dirt cheap, because they want you to stay around to gamble. Your profit model relates to both the need you meet and the way you are able to remain revenue positive.

These factors are worth examining—even if they're working very well for you—because profitability changes over time. As you prepare for Half-Retirement, you'll need to ask yourself if anything is going to change about your cost structure or cost advantages down the road. Are there any ways to save money that can offer you a meaningful competitive advantage? Consider Southwest Airlines, which came to prominence at a time when most airlines were failing to show profits and even going out of business. Their decision to keep things simple and not to offer flights to every city, not use hubs, utilize less expensive airports (e.g., Love Field instead of Dallas-Fort Worth), fly only one type of plane, and not offer meals, all enabled them to be profitable while others failed.

Your sales model relates to how easily your product or service is marketed and sold. Do you have a marketing process that is proven, documented, repeatable, and able to be sold by an average sales-person? That sales model will score much higher than one where a rock star salesperson is required in order to move any merchandise. In Half-Retirement, marketing-dependent approaches are preferred over sales intensive approaches, because they are more controllable and less people dependent. If you've ever had a rock star sales-person, you know what I mean. These folks make you a lot of money, but you are beholden to them. They control your sales, not you. In a marketing dependent model, you have better control and more freedom to Half-Retire. (There are additional lessons and resources available on our website.)

Sustainability

How sustainable is your business model? Do you realistically antic-ipate an ongoing competitive advantage into the foreseeable future, or are there disruptions visible on the horizon? Disruptions can range from a huge new technology that will shake up your industry, to something as small as a long-term contract with a major customer that is about to expire.

In addition to assessing the climate you are doing business in, you need to determine your company's innovation quotient: your own capacity and need to innovate compared to others in your industry. For instance, use of technological tools can create advan-tage, but a lawn care company that utilizes tablets to track customer workflows may or may not create a competitive advantage over one that doesn't. But a company that manufactures computer processors needs to constantly innovate just to keep pace, let alone outpace competitors. Finding out exactly where you fall between these two extremes is key to remaining competitive into the future.

You want to examine all these possibilities as realistically as you can to score your business model's sustainability. Remember, your goal is to avoid as many pitfalls as possible. Don't worry about the ones you can't control. I suggest my clients perform this scoring exercise on their business models once a year.

Rethinking Your Operations Model

Rethinking your operations model gives you an opportunity to enhance or modify systems to better serve you in Half -Retirement. If you are like most businesses, your operational systems were created many years ago and have only had a few tweaks over those years. Are those systems creating the most value for customers? Do they cement you as the low-cost provider? Can they be improved or better leveraged?

Some business owners balk at any changes, because they are reluctant to lose the organic feel and rhythm to the way things are done. But rethinking or better systematizing things is one more way to improve your Half-Retirement. The trick to this exercise is similar to Zero Based Budgeting. Use a blank slate. Just because it's the way you have done it, doesn't mean that it's the best way now. Challenge everything. Remember, your current systems were designed to have you working in them,whereas a Half-Retire system needs to be designed to work without you.

Many operations models can benefit from redesigning various processes with the goal of saving both time and money. This often involves combining steps or eliminating them altogether. You will often end up completely changing the method you use to do things, such as hiring an outside company to do payroll or sales instead of doing it in-house, or getting your customers to agree to automated credit card charges instead of sending invoices.

Before you "Yeah, but" (I like to call this a "Yabut") me, and say "How can I not send invoices?" ask yourself, "When is the last invoice you got from your health club?" The health club may invoice for internal purposes, but they autobill and skip the step of customer invoicing. This streamlined process saves them time and money. You can find similar operational opportunities if you look hard enough.

You may also locate a bottleneck step in one of your processes that is costing you time or money unnecessarily. I have a large client whose company was handling a lot of delivery receipts and confirmations. As the paper was passed from desk to desk, everyone removed the paperclip to view the various items, threw the paperclip away, and then reassembled the stack with a new paperclip. This organically created process was costing $10,000 in paperclips annually. Sometimes this kind of re-leveraging requires you to look at your processes as an outsider.

Don't forget your new mindset of pragmatism. Rethinking your operations model will involve some tradeoffs; you want to choose the tradeoffs that offer you the most time and money back, while affecting the least important parts of the business. Doing things the "best" way isn't the goal; Half-Retirement is. I like to point to credit card companies as a prime example. In the past, there were many credit card companies that had pretty mediocre customer service, but their revenues didn't really suffer. They bet (successfully) on the fact that customers would put up with a lot in order to keep a credit card with a competitive rate.

 This is proof that in some cases, "good enough" is good enough.

One of my clients ran a property management company, which was a low-margin business with a lot of day-to-day issues. After thirty years of hard work and low profits, she decided to bet heavily on technology to transform her operations model. Instead of dealing with hundreds of bank accounts to process Home Owners Association payments, she was able to offload the entire process through technology and outsourcing. This required customers to pay online (or pay a surcharge) and eliminated most of the need for human labor. She used an industry-specific bank to receive the checks and even post them to customer accounts through integration with her enterprise resource planning system (ERP). This drove down costs and drove down problems. Shifting business processes to a "technology first" approach was a completely different way of doing things from her previous three decades, but it enabled her to Half-Retire.

Another client put together kits of various imported products and sold them on an e-commerce site. They had a complex coordination of incoming products, as well as shipped a few hundred packages a day. This lead to staff devoting huge amounts of time to dealing with customer inquiries about their kits. When he was ready to Half-Retire, he made the leap to incorporate FedEx live data into their customer relations software. This required a large front-end investment on his part, but it enabled customers to check on their own orders and allowed much easier vendor integration. By managing everything with technology, he cut down on the number of people he had to manage, saving him both time and money. (The project cost $150,000 and paid for itself in fifteen months.)

Re-leveraging assets can mean completely reinventing your company or just tweaking a few things here and there. Whatever your individual situation, you can make powerful changes that will enable you to get more from your company to support your Half-Retirement!

CHAPTER 9

SETTING THE AUTOPILOT

DURING THE EARLY days of aviation, pilots had to physically steer airplanes as well as manage all the dials, gauges, and instruments at all times. Today, we take it for granted that commercial aircraft are largely managed by an autopilot system that perpetually monitors countless instruments to ensure that the plane's altitude, speed, direction, and other important variables are correct. A properly functioning autopilot enables the human pilots to focus their energy on just a handful of key instruments instead of hundreds of them. Should one of these display a warning sign, the pilots take over for the autopilot and evaluate which of the hundreds of potential issues needs their attention.

You can shift from managing with your eyes to a Half-Retire Autopilot by creating the right culture, managing from a custom-designed KPI dashboard, and creating financial controls that serve your Half-Retirement.

In Half-Retirement, you will transition from constantly monitoring your business to putting it on autopilot. This isn't necessarily complicated, but it can feel very unnatural at first. Most of us grow accustomed to "managing with our eyes," which works just fine when you're in the office all the time. But managing with your eyes is like piloting the old-fashioned way. You are taking in every possible piece of data and analyzing it individually. That's a lot of work. To Half-Retire, you will have to do better, and you can.

Creating a Half-Retire Culture

The first step to setting the autopilot is to create a Half-Retire culture that will manage the business in your stead. Culture can be defined in many different ways, but at work, it usually boils down to "the way we do things." For most businesses, there are two "the way we do things": one when you are present and one when you are away. This is a big frustration for many business owners. Sometimes, it even stops them from considering Half-Retirement. They say things like, "There's no way I can be away from the business that long. Too many things go wrong." That can be true if you haven't set up your culture to serve your Half-Retirement. If Uncle Rudy can do it, so can you.

To create your own Half-Retire culture, you want to start by assessing your cultural strengths and weaknesses and how they relate to the drivers of your business model. Also ask yourself the ways in which your business runs worse when you're not around, and the ways in which it may actually improve. For example, you may find that productivity declines when you're out of the office, and that people have less urgency about solving customer problems. However, you may also find that some people may perform better when you are gone.

Once you've answered these questions, you can decide what is lacking when you are not in the office and what are the "must have" elements. To create these elements in your new culture, you should clarify these new expectations, find ways to raise the bar, and then institutionalize each cultural element.

When you are present, you act as the "standard bearer" for how things get done. You don't need to think about it or do anything; it just happens by you being there. By deciding on your new "must haves," you can create new cultural norms that raise the expectations that match more closely those that happen naturally when you are present.

These new non-negotiables can relate to the quality of your product, customer service, levels of productivity, how coworkers treat one another, or anything else that is important to you and your business model. Once you've prioritized, you can determine which cultural habits you want to instill and reinforce.

For example, coffee shops whose business model depends on serving the highest quality product may establish a norm to brew fresh coffee every twenty minutes, whether an urn is empty or not. This reinforces the cultural norm that fresh coffee trumps the cost or the headache of making a new pot. Companies in which the business model is driven by productivity may create a cultural norm where everyone stays at work until the job is done. It doesn't need to be insisted upon, it just happens. There are things that may happen organically when you are present, but if you are going to be out of the office more, they need to be articulated, clarified, and known as "the way we do things."

One of my clients knew that highly responsive customer service was essential to his business model, so he created a customer service email hotline and a toll-free number. He added a signature at the end of every email that went out from his company that read, "If you are dissatisfied with the service you received in any way, please email our customer service manager directly or call our customer service hotline," and then gave the number. This simple step created greater accountability for everyone in the company. All his customer service representatives knew that this check was in place, and it gave them the extra motivation they needed to be patient and polite.

Culture Action Plan

Once you've selected your top priority cultural changes, you want to go about implementing them intentionally and methodically. Remember that you are turning a battleship, not a speedboat, so it's going to take some time. Here are some proven techniques to try:

1. Send a memo.

   - This very straightforward step will explain clearly exactly what changes you want to see and why. You may even want to display key points from the memo on posters as a follow-up.

2. Hold a team meeting.

   - Like a memo, the goal of a meeting is to communicate your new expectations clearly and emphatically.

3. Set up an auto-reminder.

   - You can send a regular email to remind everyone of the new cultural expectations or just add a new phrase or motto to your signature for internal communications.

4. Look for opportunities to create cultural lore.

   - You can create memorable moments if you are looking for windows of opportunity. A friend of mine owned a fast-food store whose value proposition was fresh beef, and his team let a big beef shipment stay outside too long during the lunch rush. Rather than put the perfectly good beef in the freezer to save money, the owner took the "moment" to demonstrate that they did NOT sell frozen beef...EVER. He told the team to throw all the beef in the dumpster and had the entire crew participate. That story was told and retold over the years, reinforcing the norm that they did not sell frozen beef.

5. Catch people doing something right.

- You want to affirm and recognize desirable behavior and actions, so if you see employees implementing your new expectations, praise them for it. If appropriate, you may even want to recognize them in front of their colleagues to advertise that you are noticing the positive cultural changes.

6. Catch people doing something wrong.

- If you are serious about your priorities, you have to offer consequences for not implementing them. These may just be you or a deputy pointing out the infraction now and then, or even nagging the team until they get it right. This is hard for business owners, because consistency isn't necessarily our greatest strength. Stay on it, though, and your team will figure out that you are serious and stick with it. Otherwise, they'll just give it lip service and forget.

7. Utilize KPIs.

- As we'll discuss in the next section, you can use key performance indicators to "watch" your business even when you're not there. You can also tie employee incentives to these KPIs when appropriate and productive.

Generally, it's a good idea to balance the carrot and the stick. You need both, but you don't want to go too far in one direction or the other. Your employees need to know you are serious, but they shouldn't feel berated or discouraged.

What About the Doubters?

Change is never easy, and it's completely normal to have a few team members who don't buy into the new way of doing things. Some may even try to sabotage what you are working to achieve. There isn't necessarily one right way of dealing with this, but you cannot let an employee derail your Half-Retirement. It's not their business; it's yours. You may need to talk directly to these people to clarify your determination. Give them a chance to conform. If they refuse, you may need to let them go. In some situations, you may be forced to choose between keeping a valuable employee who will not conform or sacrificing Half-Retirement.

Many clients will ask me if I think all of their employees *have* to be on board and support their Half-Retirement to make it successful. My short answer is no. Many business owners Half-Retire without their staff knowing about their goal or supporting it. Half-Retirement will be easier with your staff's help, but you can do it without them. Remember, it's your company, and it's your life, not theirs. They weren't there when you risked everything at the beginning to get your business off the ground, and it won't be their problem if you're working around the clock when you're eighty years old. Many of your employees will just want to know that their job is as secure in Half-Retirement as it was yesterday. Your employees do not need to be enthusiastic about your Half-Retirement, but they do need to perform in their new roles to support it.

Ultimately, successful Half-Retirement doesn't depend on your entire team liking or supporting the changes. Don't kid yourself that everyone is going to be happy for you, and don't try to force anyone to care. It's much more important that you demonstrate your determination and commitment to see the Half-Retirement process through completely.

All that said, you should take some steps to sell as many members of your team as possible on the Half-Retirement process. Give them the opportunity to jump on board. Point out that your impending Half-Retirement will offer a real chance for professional advancement for those who are interested. Willing and capable people will have the opportunity to develop their skills, take on more responsibility, and increase their pay. Ambitious individuals will have the chance to step up and prove themselves. Hopefully, these opportunities will help mitigate any inconvenience that the Half-Retirement changes may bring.

Culture Change in Action

A client of mine, "Jason," bought a fifty-year-old company that was about to go out of business. Jason had been a CFO for most of his career and was accustomed to leading in a command-and-control style. He was successful in taking the company—which manufactured and installed illuminated signs—and completely turning it around. He got everything well organized, implemented a good sales process, and made it profitable for the first time in years.

However, once Jasonwas ready to spend less time in the office, he had to rethink the culture he had created, which was built around him running things with an iron fist. The company still struggled with some operational and quality issues, which Jason would deal with as they came up. Customers sometimes complained that their signs wouldn't light up the night after the installer left, requiring the team to come back out and eating into their margin. Jason was used to managing these issues by his constant physical presence. That had to change.

Jason created a new norm in his company, which involved taking several pictures of the lighted sign, inside and out, once it had been completely installed. This simple step added transparency and ensured that installers never left the job site without first turning on the sign, and provided proof to the customer that the sign worked before the technician left. The new norm radically reduced the number of times they had to return to a job site—greatly increasing profitability—and Jason didn't have to be physically around for it to happen.

Sometimes—if you really want to change the culture—you have to make a scene. When I was running my manufacturing business, one of our key KPIs was order fill rate. We were constantly chasing four thousand part numbers and always had part availability issues. This pulled down our fill rate, so expediting production of some part numbers was critical to good order fill. And of course, no one but me ever could get every last part on the order.

One day I was busy in my office and delegated the task to an employee. About an hour before the order had to ship, I skimmed the ticket and saw several "missing" items that I knew we had. I started scanning the shelves and found a couple right away, which infuriated me. I started climbing up the shelving like a monkey finding parts that weren't easy to spot, while my team gathered in horror to watch. I started flinging them through the factory while yelling, "Here's another one we missed!"

It was probably dangerous to have ten-pound chunks of steel flying through the air, but I was beyond irritated. Our order fill rate went up immediately and permanently by creating this memorable cultural moment. About a year later, I overheard an employee telling a new hire, "Hey, Jim's a pretty good guy, but if he tells you to do something, don't mess around." That moment had become part of company lore, and I never had to climb those shelves again.

Use KPIs, not Your Eyes

When doctors visit a hospitalized patient, they rely on their intuition as well as routine exams to assess the patient's condition. Occasionally, something subtle will prompt them to run an extra test. And every so often, that "hunch" will end up catching something unexpected and saving a life.

But what about all the hours that doctors are *not* in the room with their patients? They rely on a variety of instruments to keep track of their patients' vital signs: blood pressure, heart rate, breathing, body temperature, and so on. If one of these numbers isn't where it should be, the nurses know to check it out and possibly call in the doctor.

Just like a doctor who isn't in the room all day, when you Half-Retire, you will lose your in-person "feel" for many different components of your business. These typically include areas like sales growth, customer retention, employee morale, and general financial controls. So, you will set up systems to monitor your company's vital signs by measuring certain key performance indicators. These will function like the machines that monitor a patient in a hospital, giving you the information you once absorbed with your physical presence.

Will running your business this way be exactly the same as being there? Of course not. But you will be surprised at how effective it can be. Managing by KPI is how enormous venture capitalist firms can run multiple companies in just a few minutes a month. A friend of mine from college was the CFO for a venture capital (VC) funded startup. Once a month, he, the president, and the COO would travel to the VC firm's headquarters with charts displaying their KPIs. They were each responsible for three numbers, which, for my friend, included measurements like labor utilization rates, average cost per hour, and certain recruiting metrics.

They each had fifteen minutes with the VC executives to explain their charts. If a metric wasn't where it was supposed to be, the executives would question them further and determine what corrective action was needed. Then they were sent back home to do their jobs. My friend and his two colleagues were doing all the work, but these VC executives were actually controlling the company, simply by getting consistent reporting on a few key metrics. If this strategy can work for a massive VC firm, it can certainly work for businesses like yours and mine.

What Makes a Good KPI?

When you talk about KPIs, many business owners immediately think about watching profit. But profit, revenue, and similar metrics are actually lagging indicators of business health. Profit is a result of the business working well, not a predictor of it. Profit and revenue are output activities that are easy to measure, but hard to control. You want your KPIs to be leading indicators of your business's condition. If your KPIs are in line, you will make profit. If not, you won't. KPIs measure input activities like business development, customer service satisfaction, and lead generation. They can be much trickier to measure, but they are the numbers you need to keep your eye on if you're going to be able to Half-Retire.

For example, if your number of new quality prospects drops 20 percent, you probably won't notice a decline in your profits for a few months, depending on the length of your sales cycle. But the eventual decline in revenue and profit will be a **result** of the decline in quality new prospects. If you are monitoring your number of new quality prospects—instead of merely watching profits—you will know something is wrong much earlier. This can enable you to take corrective action so that the initial 20 percent drop never shows up in your bottom line.

Although some important inputs to your business are notoriously difficult to quantify, the KPIs themselves must be objective and measurable. You've probably heard the saying, "What gets measured gets done," and it's true. Just ask any kid in school how much time he spends studying the stuff that he knows won't be on the test.

But just like some kids learn how to cheat on tests, some employees will figure out how to "work" the KPIs. For example, I know of a telemarketing lead generation company that began keeping statistics on its employees. Initially, executives decided to track the number of calls each employee made, thinking that more calls indicated greater productivity. As soon as the employees figured this out, however, they began calling hundreds of numbers with autodialers and just hanging up. Then the company considered the possibility that longer calls indicated a deeper discussion and therefore a better chance of a sale, so they began tracking that. But then employees began calling voicemail boxes and leaving the phone on their desk for an hour. Eventually, they found the right mix of variables to measure so they could identify cheaters as well as star performers.

Other KPIs may not directly encourage manipulation, but they may still create incentives you don't want. One owner wanted to lower his accounts payable balances, so he started monitoring them closely. His controller got stressed out and paid all of them down, but then the company was short for payroll. Another owner began monitoring the total number of units her company produced as a way to keep an eye on productivity. But her employees then began over-producing the parts that took less time per unit, which led to bloated inventory and decreased profitability in the long run.

These stories aren't an argument against using KPIs; they just remind us that we have to think through the incentives they create.

It's also important to include some regular spot checking for quality, distortions, and metrics gaming.

Be open to a little experimentation. You may find that measuring new customer sales may tell you less than measuring repeat sales or referral sales. Some clients swear that measuring the company-wide average employee tenure as the best metric of how well the company runs. You may need a couple of iterations before you figure out exactly what you should measure to ensure you are monitoring your inputs in the best possible way.

Sometimes the key measure is a little counterintuitive. I know an extremely successful owner who runs over ten auto-repair franchises. He made his non-negotiable metric the margin on each repair they performed. This meant he had to charge premium rates that could spike into the range of ridiculous and uncompetitive, but it also meant his stores were always profitable and he could pay his people well. This created a virtuous cycle that enabled him to keep talented managers, so he could spend most of his time away from the office. This owner made a conscious decision to give up certain customers who wouldn't pay the higher prices in order to run his stores the way he wanted.

Creating a KPI Dashboard

According to my pilot friends, the cockpit of a plane can have hundreds of dials and buttons. The pilots, however, only watch about five to ten at a time. As long as those are green, they can safely ignore the rest. But if one of those key indicators shows signs of trouble, it's time to investigate what's going on more deeply.

KPIs won't help you Half-Retire if you're watching too many at once, or if the ones you watch take too much time to read. Your goal is to select three to five KPIs that you can scan in a few minutes on a weekly basis. Only when one of those shows signs of trouble do you take a deeper dive.

Your dashboard should include the best KPIs that relate to the drivers of your business model. These vary greatly depending on both your industry and your niche within that industry. They could include margin, quality, customer satisfaction, growth, as well as customer acquisition and retention. Whichever ones you choose, make sure that revenues and profits follow them.

For example, if you own a retail business known for excellent customer service, you will want to monitor customer satisfaction rates. Those will predict how many customers are returning to purchase again and referring you to their friends and family members. On the other hand, if you make your money by undercutting your competitors' prices, you will need to keep a close eye on your cost centers.

Create your own short list of KPIs you want to watch as you spend more and more time away from the office. Keep them simple and straightforward, and be open to adjusting them over time. A few examples of some KPIs that are working for many companies:

1. New quality prospects generated per month

   - This requires you to develop a clear definition of a new quality prospect and measure how many you get as accurately as possible.

2. Net Promoter Score

   - This is a number you develop to express how many customers are actually happy enough to go out and promote your company to their family and friends.

3. Defect or Return Rate

   - After getting crushed by higher quality Japanese cars, Ford developed a quality score for its own products and its vendors and began watching it in order to compete more effectively.

4. Dollars of sellable margin produced per worker-hour

   - This is a more finely tuned measure of productivity, especially if your business model includes undercutting your competitors' prices.

5. Cost per customer service call

   - You want to keep your customers happy, but not at the expense of all your profits. This KPI measures the ability of your customer service representatives to keep them happy without breaking the bank.

6. The speed and accuracy of monthly financial statements

   - Lagging indicators are still important to watch, and the sooner you get them, and the more accurate they are, the more useful they are to you. One of my clients became frustrated with the sluggishness of his accounting department, so he began incentivizing getting 100 percent accurate financials by the third of each month. What gets measured gets done, and suddenly, he had the information he needed right on time.

7. Accounts Receivables and Accounts Payable Ratios

   - Many clients track the ratio of receivables to payables and Average Days of Receivables or

Payables as a way to monitor the health of their
customers, vendors, and accounting team.

8. Internal customer satisfaction ratings

    ▪ Some of my clients monitor customer satisfac-
      tion ratings internally to ensure their Google or
      Yelp ratings stay strong. By learning about issues
      sooner, they can beat complainers to the punch
      and avoid negative public reviews.

Remember, all KPIs should relate to the drivers of your business model, and they have to be measurable. For example, you
can't measure employee morale, but you can measure how many
complaints Human Resources receives. Ideally, your KPIs should be
measured daily or in real time. Like the airline pilot, you're monitoring a few details very closely, and then taking quick, corrective
action if something goes wrong.

KPI Incentives in Action

One of my clients owned a service company that effectively sold
labor, so labor efficiency was their most important KPI. When the
crew worked quickly, the company was very profitable. When they
didn't, their margins dwindled away. When the owner was ready to
Half-Retire, he was concerned that the crew could be less effective
without him closely monitoring their efficiency.

To address this concern, my client decided to switch up the
incentives. After watching his labor efficiency numbers closely for
some time, he concluded that if his crew was working at a reasonable pace, the cost of their labor on a job would be 24 percent of the
total revenue. So instead of paying everyone hourly, he told his crew
that they would get 24 percent of the job ticket, regardless of how
many hours it took.

Suddenly, the crew began to work quickly and efficiently on every job. They were especially careful to avoid mistakes that would require them to return to the job site as they would have to do it for free. The owner was able to align his interests—having satisfied customers and good labor efficiency—with his crew's interest in maximizing their hourly rate. The shift enabled him to manage them without actually being around.

Creating Flash Reports

Flash reports are snapshots of your important KPIs and other data you want to see regularly. In Half-Retirement, your staff will produce them for you on a weekly or monthly basis. A good flash report—like the ones my college friend was required to bring to his VC firm—should be easy to scan so you can quickly determine if anything needs further attention. If you can't look at it and get the information you need in a couple of minutes, find ways to simplify it until you can. Think red light, green light, not deep analysis or thought.

Don't worry if your flash reports take your employees some time to prepare, especially at first. Remember the 10X rule from the previous chapter? Charts and graphics are fine, as long as they aid in your ease of reading and absorbing the information. Remember, Half-Retirement is about enabling you to see what's going on, while saving you time. (We have examples of flash reports and resources to help you design your own on our website.)

It's vital that you have your flash reports generated on a regular basis, ideally at every meeting you attend. Even if you hear complaints, this is one area that's non-negotiable. When one of my client's employees mentioned they hadn't gotten around to generating the flash report, he stopped the meeting and told them it would reconvene when they got it done. Do this once or twice, and over time, you will get the team onboard and develop a rhythm to your flash reporting.

Financial Controls

I apologize in advance for bringing up this unpleasant topic. If I had a nickel for every time I have heard, "Jim, I can trust my staff with my life," I would have a lot of nickels. However, I have also seen family members of clients steal millions or engage in shady side deals. I have seen sweet grandma types that everyone loved disappear in the middle of the night with all the company cash. One of my favorites is a CFO who used company funds to build seven hotels. He paid back every dime, but put millions of company dollars at risk. Trust is great, but trust works much better when employees know you will find out if they are up to no good.

Even if you trust your entire staff implicitly, you need solid financial controls in order to Half-Retire. There are endless reasons for this. You will be around a lot less, which makes fraud and expensive mistakes more likely. You will probably hire new employees who don't know you as well, nor feel the sense of loyalty to you that others do. And you never know what is going on in people's lives that might drive them to defraud or embezzle when they would normally never consider such an act.

For all these reasons, you will want to keep a close eye on your financial data throughout your Half-Retirement. However, that data is only as good as your people's ability and willingness to enter it correctly. This means that you will have to learn to think like a thief in order to avoid being victimized by one.

Think Like a Thief

What's the worst that could happen if you try to Half-Retire without setting these financial controls? Let me give you just a few real-life examples:

- An employee taps the company line of credit for half a million dollars and leaves the country.

188

- An employee collects the receivables, but never marks them as paid. You think you've got several unpaid invoices out there, while your employee is spending the money.

- An employee pockets some payments and never records the transactions. I knew of a receptionist at a doctor's office who collected all the copays and deposited them into her personal bank account using her phone. This is also a tremendous risk in businesses with lots of cash transactions.

- An employee creates a bank account with a similar name and deposits checks written to your company into hers or his.

- An employee creates a different company and begins billing customers under the "sister" company, pocketing the revenue.

- An employee creates a phony vendor that begins receiving payments from your company.

- An employee uses company funds to pay personal bills (for example, by placing a personal cellphone bill on the company credit card).

- An employee brings his own cash register to work and carries it home with all the cash at the end of the shift. (This happened to a major retailer!)

- An employee gives him or herself a raise.

Incoming and Outgoing Funds

It's impossible to make fraud impossible during Half-Retirement, but there are many policies you can implement that will make it far less likely. First, require at least two people to handle all incoming financial transactions. No single person should have access to both accounts receivable and the receipt of funds accounts, which means that the person who receives the checks is not the person who logs them into the accounting software. This builds accountability into your operations model and greatly reduces the likelihood that one person will be able to slip something into his pocket (digitally or literally) without someone else noticing.

Of course, these precautions have become much trickier in the era of online banking. The receptionist I mentioned above who was stealing copays from the doctor's office where she worked simply snapped a picture of all the checks. They weren't made out to her, but she was able to steal nearly $9,000 a month this way. When she was finally caught, the bank said there was nothing they could do. Experts tell me that most banks simply don't have the capacity to verify checks under $10,000. Yes, you are reading that right! Many banks do not verify payees or check details manually if the check is under $10,000.

As part of monitoring your outgoing funds, you should get the bank statements first emailed to your personal email account (that no one else has access to) or mailed to your home. Make sure that you at least skim these statements every month. Put limits on how much can be spent out of each account daily, and make sure that any company checks have similar restrictions. I would suggest that only you have the ability to tap into the company's line of credit.

I counsel all my clients to avoid having a rubber stamp with their signature on it. It is better to pre-sign checks with conditions ("Not to exceed $5,000," and so forth) than to leave a stamp with your legal signature that allows you to be held legally liable for anything it appears on. Lastly, you must learn your accounting software well enough to explore your accounts without help from anyone else. The very possibility that you could be poking around will make irregularities far less likely to occur.

Acid Test

Lastly, you should perform an acid test on your business regularly, making sure your income statement flows properly to the balance sheet. Most business owners skip the balance sheet and only look at the income statement. Have you ever noticed that your banker never asks for the income statement first? They always want the balance sheet. Here's why: income flows to the balance sheet. If you're only looking at your income statement, you're not seeing the full picture.

Think of it this way: your profit only lands in a few places in your balance sheet. If you take in $100,000 one month, you should see that money show up in increased cash or receivables, the purchase of assets, reduced debt or accounts payable, or dividends. If the changes in these amounts don't add up to $100,000, where did the money go? This is one of the easiest ways to catch a thief or problems with your accounting department because profit will not land in one of these places.

Setting the autopilot on your business can be scary, especially at first. It's easy to worry that the plane will crash the minute you stop steering manually. But in time, you will find that—with a healthy culture, good KPIs, and sound financial controls—you can control your business very effectively during Half-Retirement.

CHAPTER 10

MASTERING AND ENJOYING HALF-RETIREMENT

"THAT SOUNDS PERFECT for me! I'm in!"

I've heard those words countless times over the years, from thousands of business owners who are truly enthusiastic about the idea of Half-Retirement. They learn about the ideas and techniques you've just read about, and they're ready to jump right in. They possess remarkable talent and an admirable work ethic, yet not all of them are able to make Half-Retirement a reality. Why?

In my experience, there are two major reasons people succeed in Half-Retirement. First, they embrace education *and* combine it with action. They absorb the principles and the mindsets of Half-Retirement, and take the steps to transform their business into a Half-Retirement-compatible enterprise.

Successful Half-Retirees avoid a common pitfall, being too busy running their business to take the crucial steps needed. No matter how much enthusiasm you feel for the concept of Half-Retirement, implementing the system can feel a bit like changing the tire on a moving car. Successful Half-Retirees find a way to do it instead of using it as an excuse.

So, how do you pull this off? You must change how you run your business. Currently, your business runs a certain way and you have a certain role. To Half-Retire, you will need to hit the pause button long enough to create a new business process—and a new role for yourself—that serves Half-Retirement. Once you have this new business process in place and have set the autopilot, you're very, very close to the finish line. But you're not quite done. In order to truly master and enjoy the Half-Retire system, you still have to watch out for some pitfalls and make needed adjustments. I hate to even bring up this topic, but there is a real problem for Half-Retirees. They have been on "the grind" so long, and the gains they make in Half-Retirement are so powerful, that sometimes they fall into a trap from over-exuberance.

Common Pitfalls in Half-Retirement Planning

You've probably heard the fable about how to cook a live frog: you slowly increase the temperature of the water until the frog is boiled to death. If you dropped the frog directly into hot water, it would jump out, of course. But by turning the stove up gradually, you lull it into complacency.

The daily demands of your business are gradually turning the temperature of the stove up on you as the days to enjoy the spoils of your hard work slip away. Half-Retirement offers us a way to jump out of the pot. Still, there are many different traps that try to keep us in the water. Here are the most common ones I encounter:

The Ostrich

Ostriches are so excited about Half-Retirement, and so eager for it to go smoothly, that they bury their heads in the sand when those "Fix Me" signs appear on their business. Ostriches feel great in the short term, because they plow through many of their early Half-Retirement tasks very quickly. The leftover momentum from when they were more involved will often carry the business for several months without any issues. But if they don't perform those "Forever Fixes" to the problems that will naturally arise during the Half-Retirement

193

process, their company will eventually run out of steam. Remember, successful Half-Retirement is about transforming your business, not just checking off items on a list.

The Hot Potato

Hot Potatoes learn about Half-Retirement and immediately catch the part about working less. But instead of embracing fractional delegation, rethinking their business model, and strengthening their systems, they start treating work like a hot potato. They duck it, toss it to others, and generally do all they can to avoid it. As you can imagine, this becomes a form of traditional delegation, or worse, abdication, which ends up failing for all the reasons we outlined earlier in the book.

The Ghost

Ghosts take the hot potato pitfall to the next level and just stop showing up at the office. Instead of performing a calculated stress test on their business after careful planning, they just take off for a month and say, "I'm sure my team can handle things." They ignore the process of Half-Retirement and try to skip directly to the rewards. They forget about gradual graduation, thinking that everything will work itself out on its own. At best, Ghosts end up having to go back to work and start the Half-Retirement process over. At worst, they return to the office to deal with major fraud or embezzlement.

The Enabler

Enablers are also trying to skip steps in Half-Retirement, but their strategy is to install a mini-me in their place to do all their work. They forget that no matter how talented or bright the new deputy is, he or she cannot possibly have accumulated all the knowledge and experience that they have over the decades they've been running the business.

 Please keep in mind, you are doing the work you do *for a reason*. Most likely, that reason is that you fill an important role and possess skills vital to the success of your enterprise. You have designed the system to leverage these skills, and you can't just pretend your contribution is unimportant and walk out. To Half-Retire, you will need to redesign the work process to function well without you.

When the mini-me turns out to be unqualified to take the reins of the business immediately, Enablers go into denial mode, convincing themselves that they can somehow make it work. But there are tremendous risks to leaving an underqualified mini-me in charge, including pushing out important employees and making all sorts of bad business decisions, from damaging the business model to destroying the sales pipeline. By the time the Enabler realizes how many things have gone wrong, it's impossible to squeeze the toothpaste back into the tube.

The Slowpoke

The one thing Ostriches, Hot Potatoes, Ghosts, and Enablers have in common is that they are all in a rush. Slowpokes are the opposite. They know they need to Half-Retire, but they don't have any sense of urgency about it. We all have a finite number of good working years left, and if we don't move through the Half-Retirement steps thoroughly *and* promptly, we're going to run out of time.

I met a woman in San Diego who was a classic Slowpoke. She learned about the Half-Retire system, agreed completely that it was what she needed, and committed to get started right away. Mentally, she began Half-Retiring immediately. But the day-to-day demands of the business kept her in perpetual Half-Retiring mode as she could never do much more than daydream about Half-Retirement. After two years on the do-it-herself plan, she had made no measurable progress. She kept telling herself she would get around to her Half-Retirement work, but somehow, she could never do more than little bits at a time. Ultimately, these little bits added up to nothing.

This woman failed at Half-Retirement because she was on the "Whenever I get around to it" plan. This is code for "I will work on my Half-Retirement dead last." If you don't put your most important priority first, you can end up like her. So beware! This is where a Half-Retire Coach can act as a positive trap. Just like a personal trainer helps you work out better and show up for your workout, a Half-Retire Coach will help you speed through Half-Retiring much faster.

Measuring Your Progress

The key to avoiding all of these pitfalls is to regularly and comprehensively measure your progress in Half-Retirement. Even though you will see some powerful results early in the Half-Retire process, all of us can get discouraged with long-term projects at times. Whether it's losing weight or renovating a kitchen, there are days when it feels like it will never be done. Measuring your progress regularly enables you to celebrate victories while holding yourself accountable for moving the ball. Measuring your progress comprehensively prevents you from rushing haphazardly through your list and holds you accountable for being thorough. Here are the benchmarks you should see within weeks and months, not years:

1. A noticeable reduction of work

   - Despite the Hot Potato pitfall, any reduction in work is a step in the right direction. Some days, you may feel overwhelmed by your Half-Retire punch list. Those are times when it is important to remind yourself of all those little, annoying tasks you're not doing anymore. Even a half-day off every Friday is a major step up from being chained to your desk all week.

2. Key business processes working with minimal input from you

   - Developing and improving your business processes is key to getting yourself out of the office, so pay close attention to your current role in that progress. Once you have key systems functioning well, you can begin to use the time you spend at work more efficiently, and eventually reduce it even further. (More on this in the next section.)

3. Noticeable employee growth

   - One of the more gratifying benchmarks for most business owners is seeing their employees pleasantly surprise them with their ability to handle added responsibility and authority. Like a proud parent, you can take satisfaction in investing in the personal and professional development of people who are near and dear to you.

4. Not feeling needed

- After your processes and people have been in Half-Retire mode for a while, you may find that you don't really feel needed at the office anymore. This can be jarring after feeling essential for so long, but it's cause for celebration. It's all part of the plan, and don't worry, your Picasso Work© is still vital. You just have far more time to enjoy your life in the process.

5. Autopilot set and trusted

- Setting the autopilot and perfecting its function takes time. Once you can trust it to do what it's supposed to do, you are officially Half-Retired.

Strengthening Your Business Processes and Systems

We've already discussed the importance of creating and documenting systems for all your business processes. Once you've set the autopilot, you will need to revisit most of these and make some adjustments. As you go through to tweak and strengthen your systems, keep the following principles in mind:

1. You own your systems and they don't quit

- Having a system that enables any employee to do a good job is far superior to just having one or two employees who do a great job, until they quit. Of course, in a perfect world, you'll have both. But in Half-Retirement, your systems take priority.

2. Systems and culture create the environment

- I like to remind clients that you cannot directly control how your employees behave, but you can control the environment they operate in. This environment is created by your culture and your systems. As we discussed in the last chapter, positive peer pressure can do wonders to increase both productivity and quality, even when you're not physically around.

3. Incomplete training excuses underperformance

- If we are truly honest, we know that the reason we excuse employees who underperform in their responsibilities is because we know that we do not have a great process and we have not fully trained them to do their jobs. These take time and energy, but once you have done it thoroughly, you can demand the best from your team while knowing that you are being fair and reasonable.

4. Software offers its own system

- Although many owners balk at using software to handle various business processes, software is a system in itself. The right software requires users to follow a uniform set of steps and produces predictable results, which is exactly what you want out of any system. Good software greatly reduces human error and makes mistakes easier to catch. So be sure to consider software as you're strengthening your Half-Retirement systems.

5. Systems can always be improved

- There are always those employees who can find a way to mess up, even when they're working within a perfectly good system. As you're mastering Half-Retirement, you will move from having good systems to having foolproof systems. There is only so much you can design and plan ahead of time, so the way to fool-proof your systems is to watch and see which problems actually come up and adjust the system to make it unlikely to happen next time.

Remember Gradual Graduation!

As you are mastering Half-Retire, remember the principle of gradual graduation that we discussed way back in chapter 3. You will have weeks that you make so much progress you can hardly contain your enthusiasm. You will have weeks where it feels like not much has improved. This isn't going to happen all at once, but it is going to happen if you keep working at it!

There are several keys to success at this stage. First, keep a target list of all the work you are offloading at any given time. Check off each task you are able to get rid of successfully, and be sure to remind yourself how far you've come.

Second, keep that magnet strong! Visualize what you will be doing instead of the work you are offloading. Think about all your Half-Retirement activities as well as your Picasso Work©: the reason you're staying in the game at all.

Lastly, continually celebrate all your progress. Be sure to reward yourself for everything you accomplish, no matter how small. I think it's particularly meaningful when the reward is tied to the accomplishment itself, such as buying a sports car with the money saved or taking a vacation with the time you've bought back.

Remember, the principle of gradual graduation feeds that virtuous cycle of getting time and energy back, investing that time and energy in more Half-Retirement work, and then getting even more time and energy back. Build up that momentum and let it carry you over the finish line.

Build and Maintain a Strong Support System

Half-Retirement can be incredibly rewarding, but on any given day, it may not be easy. This means you need to surround yourself with people who will encourage you as you go through the process. Don't try to go it alone. Make sure that you share your progress and challenges with supportive friends and family, as well as members of the Half-Retire community if you so choose. Our Half-Retire community has other business owners like you sharing their successes and struggles, as well as a team of coaches to help business owners achieve their dream to Half-Retire.

By the same token, don't bother to discuss Half-Retirement issues with people who are critical or negative. Not everyone gets it. Some may be jealous of your success, while others just don't understand how stressful and draining running a business can be. This doesn't mean you can't be friends with people like that, of course. It just means that you will focus on the other things you have in common.

Celebrate Milestones

Business owners are the hardest-working people I know, but they stink at pausing to celebrate, because they are always pushing for the next accomplishment.

Don't downplay your success in moving towards Half-Retirement. Your smarts, hard work, and determination has made these rewards possible, and you deserve to enjoy them.

I encourage clients to set milestones during the Half-Retirement process and share them with people you care about. They will help you stay on track, because they want you to succeed, and they will probably be helping you enjoy those rewards.

Bottom line—be good to yourself during this process, and savor the process and the rewards it brings.

Enjoy!

Now comes the best part of all: enjoy yourself! This is the final step in Half-Retirement, the awards ceremony after the race has been run. Don't allow yourself to feel guilty for drawing the same salary you've drawn in the past for doing much less work. Just think of it as back pay for all that unpaid overtime you put in during the early years.

Now it's time to live your life the way you always dreamed. Spend time with your loved ones. Take your dream vacation. Take up a new hobby or put more time into the ones you already have. And most of all, just rest and relax. You've put in the work, and you've earned it.

RESOURCES

Bonus Resources

I have created a resource page available only to book readers. Here you can find downloadable resources and other valuable bonus items. Find these resources at www.halfretire.com/resources.

Example affirmations

Affirmations are a great way to change your mindset. Below are several common mindset themes and potential affirmations you can use to moidy them.

Theme: Only I can do it

- I am an expert fractionalize and have identified my Picasso Work©.

- I work to train and empower others to do work that is outside my Picasso Work©.

- All my talents and skills were learned. Others can learn them, too.

- I spend my time teaching others to do work as well as I can do it.

- When I am out of time, anyone with more time can usually do things better.

Theme: No one does it as well/fast as me

- When a highly-skilled person like me does a low-level task, I am over-delivering. My customers deserve the best the organization has...within reason.

- Everything is important but not urgent. My most urgent task is Half-Retirement, not this email/call/task.

- No one will ever be able to do things as fast as me, but if they can do something correctly, it's one less thing I need to do.

- I measure the speed I can get out the door, not the speed I accomplish a task.

Theme: Why can't my people think more like an owner/me?

- I am the only owner of this business and am the only one who will think like an owner...and that's fine.

- It's my people's job to complete their tasks quickly and correctly, not to think like an owner.

- My business needs great people who do a great job at their assigned tasks.

- I have thoroughly strategized the next year, so my people don't need to. They only need to execute the strategy.

Theme: The only person at the company with permission to fail is you

- I give my people all the tools and information they need to make great decisions.

- I give my people permission to fail.

- I trust my people to make decisions as if it were their business.

Theme: Perfectionism

- I do high-quality work but know when to stop at the point of diminishing returns.

- We do high-quality work but know when to stop at the point of diminishing returns.

- I know that the cost of perfectionism is less fun in Half-Retirement.

Theme: A personal or corporate culture of urgency

- Dependability and speed are two things, not one.

- I can be a 'get things done' kind of person without action items getting done instantly.

- I pride myself on getting things done in a timely matter.

- I balance time efficiency and urgency well.

- We operate quickly and efficiently without excessive stress or pressure.

Theme: Needing to be busy

- My work protects my passive investment in the business.

- I make money from the business, whether I show up or not.

- I have spent X years growing this business; my "dues" are already paid.

Theme: I need to set a good example for my employees, or they won't work hard

- It's my employee's job to do their job, not critique mine (to counteract "I need to set an example for my employees).

- They are going to do what they are going to do, and I'm going to do what I'm going to do.

- Employees will never fully understand all the toil I put into this business, and it doesn't matter. What does matter is them doing their job well.

Theme: Hard work moves me closer to my goal

- Getting my task list down to only my Picasso Work© is best for the organization and me.

- I work hard and efficiently, doing only the work I can do.

- I only work on the tasks that move me closer to Half-Retirement.

Theme: Trust as a shortcut for systems

- I always trust but verify.

- I have great KPIs and trust them to find issues early.

- Trust can be earned and unearned.

- I know that trusting for convenience's sake risks my Half-Retirement.

- I am constantly improving our systems.

Theme: An organizational structure built with the owner at the center of everything

- I feel sorry for the person in this cartoon

- Every time my employees come to me with "What do you think?" I know that answering the question hinders my Half-Retirement.

- I love the action of business, but I love the action of _____ more.

PEOPLE YOU NEED ON YOUR HALF-RETIREMENT TEAM

- A financial planner who understands Half-Retirement. Not all financial planners are created equally. Many financial planners understand how small business works and small business owners think. Many of these financial planners also understand Half-Retirement and it's implications on your business, your finances, and your life. Don't settle for someone who doesn't get what you are trying to accomplish in Half-Retirement.

- A coach or consultant can be helpful to navigate any difficult changes you may make. Working side-by-side with a business expert can greatly speed your progress towards Half-Retirement. If you would like to work with a Certified Half-Retire Coach, you can find one at https://halfretire.com/find-a-coach/.

- An expert in the exit planning arena can be helpful in some circumstances. These experts understand the options and ramifications of exiting a business. Many of them understand Half-Retirement can be a better option than a traditional exit and can advise you how to meet all of your goals. Be careful to make sure your Exit Planner understands Half-Retirement, or you could get directed towards a "canned solution" simply because the advisor is unaware of Half-Retirement.

- A supportive friend or family member can help you if the going gets tough, or you just need someone to hear you vent. Most people default to their spouse or significant other for this role. I'd recommend someone else if possible. Your life partner wants to enjoy the benefits of Half-Retirement, not hear the issues. Your partner is probably a better choice for the "pusher" role than the supportive role.

- Someone who cares enough to push you. We all need that person who can remind us to dig a little deeper. Spouses or life partners are great for reminding us that we promised to go to Italy next spring. Those positive traps help to keep moving towards Half-Retirement. If you occasionally need a kick in the rear, a good business coach or Half-Retire coach can help.

TIME LOG

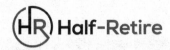

ime Log

Category	Monday	Tuesday	Wednesday	Thursday	Friday	Total
Administration						
Sales/Marketing						
Accounting/ Finance						
Emails						
Meetings						
Personal						
Unscheduled Interruptions						
Other:						
Total Proactive Time						
Total Reactive Time						

Instructions:
- Pre-printed categories are just examples. Create your own to best reflect your time commitments.
- 1 tick mark for every 15 minutes
- Approximation is fine. This is not meant to be time consuming
- Use no more than 10 categories
- The purpose of the exercise is to discover patterns, not exactly categorize your time
- It is more difficult to offload proactive work than reactive work. Tracking your time in each broad category can be helpful.

JENGA ASSESSMENT

Half-Retire® Cheat Sheet

HR Half-Retire

Complete the "Jenga Test" for every function of the business

Perform the Jenga Test for all areas of your business

	Runs well Without Me								Jenga topples Wihtout Me
Accounting/Finance/Legal	1	2	3	4	5	6	7	8	9	10
Detail									
Purchasing/Inventory	1	2	3	4	5	6	7	8	9	10
Detail									
Business Planning & Strategy	1	2	3	4	5	6	7	8	9	10
Detail									
Sales	1	2	3	4	5	6	7	8	9	10
Detail									
Marketing	1	2	3	4	5	6	7	8	9	10
Detail									
Engineering/Design	1	2	3	4	5	6	7	8	9	10
Detail									
Manufacturing/Production	1	2	3	4	5	6	7	8	9	10
Detail									

Perform the Jenga Test for all areas of your business

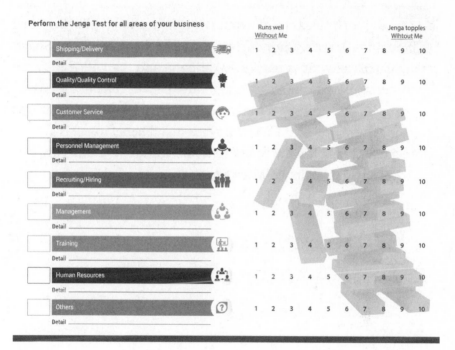

		Runs well Without Me								Jenga topples Wihtout Me	
Shipping/Delivery		1	2	3	4	5	6	7	8	9	10
Detail											
Quality/Quality Control		1	2	3	4	5	6	7	8	9	10
Detail											
Customer Service		1	2	3	4	5	6	7	8	9	10
Detail											
Personnel Management		1	2	3	4	5	6	7	8	9	10
Detail											
Recruiting/Hiring		1	2	3	4	5	6	7	8	9	10
Detail											
Management		1	2	3	4	5	6	7	8	9	10
Detail											
Training		1	2	3	4	5	6	7	8	9	10
Detail											
Human Resources		1	2	3	4	5	6	7	8	9	10
Detail											
Others		1	2	3	4	5	6	7	8	9	10
Detail											

ACKNOWLEDGMENTS

THANKS TO THE many clients and colleagues that helped formulate and refine the ideas that became Half-Retire. Robert Bogue, Doug Hall, Yolanda Harris, Chuck Ryerson, Bill Schoeffler, Steve Shaer, Mike Struzik, Fred Sussman, Jeff Wolfberg, and my wife Beth were my sounding boards and helped separate the wheat from the chaff.

Many clients jumped into the Half-Retire program while it was still under development. Their innovation and belief in me is greatly appreciated. There are too many to name, but extra thanks are due to Gerry Golden, Rex Jones, Mike Kuepper, and Lesley Stoeffler.